Learn Mandarin Chinese for Beginners

A Step-by-Step Guide to Master the
Chinese Language Quickly and Easily
While Having Fun

Leo W. Chang

Download the Audio Book Version of This Book for FREE

If you love listening to audio books on-the-go, I have great news for you. You can download the audio book version of this book for FREE just by signing up for a FREE 30-day audible trial! See below for more details!

Audible Trial Benefits

As an audible customer, you will receive the below benefits with your 30-day free trial:

- FREE audible book copy of this book
- After the trial, you will get 1 credit each month to use on any audiobook
- Your credits automatically roll over to the next month if you don't use them
- Choose from Audible's 200,000 + titles
- Listen anywhere with the Audible app across multiple devices
- Make easy, no-hassle exchanges of any audiobook you don't love
- Keep your audiobooks forever, even if you cancel your membership
- And much more

Write this text in your browser or scan the code!

For Audible US https://gat.to/vsl91

For Audible UK https://gat.to/na01j

contained within this document, including, but not limited to, errors, omissions, or inaccuracies.

Table of Contents

Introduction

The decision to pick up another language is not an easy one. Many want to learn Mandarin but look at the traditional style of writing and automatically think it is too difficult. This is where congratulations is necessary, as you took the next step into learning a language that is revolutionizing the world as we know it. No matter what your reasoning is for wanting to learn Mandarin, this book will be with you every step of the way, guiding you through the easiest ways to learn Mandarin in manners that are fun and educational.

Coupled with this book is a workbook that will provide you with hands -on practice for learning to both read and write Mandarin. It will teach you the order of brush strokes, how some Mandarin characters were created, as well as their meaning. But first, one needs to delve into a bit of history, as that is where true interest is cultivated.

Mandarin has been an important language throughout history, from its use as morse code in wars to its role in communicating assassination notices. Mandarin has become ingrained within modern society, with more individuals wanting to learn the language than ever before.

In 2016, a study was done by Global Exam, where they recorded 40 million students learning and preparing for the Hanyu Shuiping Kaoshi (HSK), also written in Mandarin as 汉语水平考试, which is a test that evaluates Mandarin language proficiency. The Global Exam further mentioned that they expect a number of no less than 100 million students learning to prepare for the HSK in 2020, a number that has been exceeded.

Embedded within Mandarin are a bunch of different meanings. What is meant by this is that as you start to learn about the different tones in

Mandarin, especially those related to pinyin, you will begin to understand the intricacies of the language. A different tone given the same character can easily have a completely alternate meaning. That's why this book has been carefully structured in order to ensure that readability is maximized.

With the Mandarin language having many little intricacies that need to be effectively understood, for example, the direction of brush strokes when writing Mandarin characters, it can seem rather difficult when starting off. However, this book is written by those who understand the difficulties of the Mandarin language, as well as the pitfalls that many fall into when learning the language. This is exactly what this book aims to ameliorate.

Although we want you all to learn and be as fluent in Mandarin as you can possibly be, it will not happen overnight. Learning a new language will take lots of time, repetition and dedication. What you put in, is what you will get out. This book intends to act as a resource that creates a strong foundation for learning Mandarin. You may find that as you progress, you start to forget the basics. This is one of the reasons that *Learn Mandarin Chinese for Beginners* was created—to ensure that your basic Mandarin skills are always top-notch.

A memory that reinforced the creation of this book was my own journey in learning Mandarin. The excitement of booking your next HSK test was often coupled with a large number of sleepless nights before the test. The amount of time I had used to focus on the repetition, speech, and characters could probably have earned me a good sum of money.

However, the feeling of passing and receiving your HSK certificate, allowing you to move on to the next level, is such a surreal feeling. You see, Mandarin is more than just memorizing a bunch of characters; it integrates history with current teachings, ensuring that the cultural aspect of the Mandarin language is not mitigated.

You have taken the first step in learning Mandarin. Remember the level of excitement that you are currently feeling. Ensure that you stay motivated and dedicated to your own learning, as it is with self-discipline that you will be conversing in Mandarin with all of your friends. Whether you are learning Mandarin as a party trick, because you find Chinese culture interesting, or you are planning to immigrate to an Asian country that speaks Mandarin, the journey starts now.

Chapter 1:

The History of Mandarin

Understanding the history of Mandarin will allow you to appreciate the development of the language from many different dynasties to the dialect of Mandarin that we utilize today. With Mandarin being the official language of both mainland China, as well as Taiwan, it does not mean that it is not spoken in other countries around the world. Singapore and many other countries of the United Nations recognize Mandarin as one of their official languages. With that being said, it is currently the most widely-spoken language across the world.

As with many languages that are ingrained in history, there is a rather large multitude of dialects that exist. Dialects are not languages per se, and are rather seen as a subset of a language that is spoken in a specific city or country. There are many different versions of Mandarin that are spoken in the various provinces within China. For example, in Hong Kong, Cantonese, a specific dialect of Mandarin, is spoken.

Many times, there are only subtle differences in the different dialects, which can thankfully be identified in their written form since they can be quite confusing for new learners. The reason for this identification is that the standard Mandarin characters are used when communicating in the written form, which heightens the degree to which those conversing understand each other, even though their spoken dialects are mutually unintelligible.

Believe it or not, there are what we call language families and groups. Mandarin is a part of the Chinese family of languages, which is seen as a subsection of the Sino-Tibetan language group. Ever since the beginning of Mandarin's creation, it has been labeled the tonal language, meaning that the manner in which specific characters are pronounced will dictate their meaning. With Mandarin having four tones, some other languages that fall under the Chinese language family have up to ten distinct tones. This means that when we hear the word "Mandarin", we need to tread with caution as it actually has two meanings when used to refer to language.

Mandarin can refer to a specific language group or as its better-known reference, being that of the Beijing dialect of mainland China's standard language. To create some context, the Mandarin language group includes both standard Mandarin (mainland China's official language), and Jin (also referred to as Jin-yu), a language spoken by occupants of inner Mongolia and the central-north region of China.

When referring to *Language Atlas of China*, there is a division whereby eight different dialects are spoken. How these eight divisions differ is via the manner that the Middle Chinese entering tone is utilized. In order to provide some geographical context, we have included the eight divisions below:

- Northeastern Mandarin is spoken by approximately 98 million individuals. Typically, this form of Mandarin is spoken in all places of Manchuria except in the Liaodong Peninsula. Since there is a very strong similarity with standard Chinese, there are very few tonal differences that establish a differentiation.

- Beijing Mandarin is spoken by approximately 27 million individuals. Typically spoken in Beijing along with in Chengde and Northern Hebei, it has begun to branch further into areas such as northern Xinjiang. With the Beijing dialect forming the basis of standard Chinese, one would expect there to be more individuals who speak it. However, it is because many researchers group Beijing Mandarin and Northeastern Mandarin together based on similarity that the number of people who speak these two dialects respectively are combined.

- Jilu Mandarin is localized to the Hebei and Shandong provinces, with approximately 89 million individuals speaking this dialect. There are marked differences regarding the tones and vocabulary when compared to standard Chinese, leading to zero understanding when conversing with the latter.

- Jiao Liao Mandarin shows a very large degree of variance when compared to Beijing Mandarin. Typically, this variance has resulted in only 35 million individuals speaking the dialect. With very noticeable changes in tone, it is primarily spoken by the Shandong and Liaodong Peninsulas.

- Central Plains Mandarin, spoken by approximately 186 million individuals, is typically found in the central parts of Shaanxi, eastern Gansu, and southern Xinjiang. There is . marked intelligibility when compared to Beijing Mandarin, primarily due to the phonological differences.

- Lanyin Mandarin is spoken by 17 million individuals across the central and western Gansu province, as well as in the Ningxia autonomous region.

- Lower Yangtze Mandarin is spoken in Jiangsu and Anhui by approximately 86 million individuals. Typically, there are marked phonological and lexical differences, establishing a sense of intelligibility when compared to Beijing Mandarin.

- A dialect spoken by approximately 260 million individuals is Southwestern Mandarin. Spoken by the Guizhou, Yunnan, Sichuan and Hubei provinces, the sharp tonal, phonological, and lexical changes establish marked intelligibility with Beijing Mandarin.

As history progressed, the term "Mandarin" was initially used by the Portuguese to refer to Imperial Chinese court magistrates when referring to the language that they spoke. However, as Mandarin moved closer toward the Western world, the Chinese themselves starting referring to the language as pǔtōng huà (普通话), guó yǔ (国语), or huá yǔ (華语). Delving deeper into these three variants, pǔ tōng huà directly translates to "common language", referring to the language´ that is spoken by inhabitants of mainland China. Guó yǔ means "national language" and is used by those in Taiwan, with huá yǔ also having the same meaning, but it is used by those residing in Singapore and Malaysia.

Delving a bit deeper into the history of Mandarin, many have the following question: How did Mandarin actually become China's official language? Given its geographical size, China consists of a wide variety of different languages and dialects. However, it was in the Ming Dynasty (1368 - 1644) that Mandarin emerged as the language of choice by the ruling class.

The Beijing dialect became associated with Mandarin in the latter part of the Ming Dynasty. China's capital changed from Nanjing to Beijing, remaining as Beijing throughout the Ming and Qing Dynasties. With Mandarin being the language of the ruling class, it naturally became the language of choice in courts, as well as amongst the public who were interacting with these courts. Officials from different provinces in China continued to migrate to mainland China, needing to adapt their dialects in order to communicate in court. However, it was not until 1909 that Mandarin became the national language of China.

Typically, when a dynasty falls, there is a change in the main language of the country. However, when the Qing dynasty fell in 1912, Mandarin remained the main language utilized in the Republic of China. To commemorate the fall of the Qing Dynasty, it was renamed as pǔ tōng huà in 1955. Although this renaming was adopted by most of the countries that used Mandarin as an official language, some countries like Taiwan continue to refer to Mandarin as guó yǔ.

Mandarin uses Chinese characters, known as Hànzì (漢字), as its writing system, however, these characters have their own history. Chinese characters appeared over 2,000 years ago, represented as images of real objects. However, as time progressed, the characters became more stylized and started representing ideas as well as objects. With that being said, many characters can comprise two or more ideas, all illustrated differently based on the direction and amount of brush strokes present.

Each Chinese character represents a specific syllable of the Chinese language. However, it needs to be acknowledged that there are many Chinese characters that cannot be used independently as they wouldn't make sense on their own. It is usually the Chinese writing system that deters individuals from wanting to learn Mandarin. However, although it definitely has a certain complexity about it, there are many modern-day tips that can be used to master this writing system.

According to the *Kangxi Dictionary* (康熙字典), there are 47,035 Chinese characters. With there being quite a few historical Chinese character formations that were possibly not registered in the *Kangxi Dictionary*, the actual number to this day remains a mystery. However, do not let this number scare you, as there are really only 3,500 basic Chinese characters that are used for everyday communication. As everything does, Chinese characters have evolved over thousands of years. Their scripts and styles have been changed to form what we now know as freehand cursive, or Xing Shu (行書).

Oracle bone inscriptions were the first depictions of Chinese characters, and they were typically seen as inscriptions on the carapaces of mammals and tortoises during the Shang Dynasty (1600 - 1046 BCE). These inscriptions were typically used for divination, leading it to being called "bu ci" (卜辭).

With there being approximately 4,000 different inscriptions recorded in history, only a thousand of them have successfully been deciphered. As the Shang Dynasty led into the Zhou Dynasty (1046 - 256 BCE), bronze inscriptions were noticed on ritual wine vessels and other bronze objects. There were a further 4,000 different bronze inscriptions present, with more than half of them being successfully understood today.

As the Zhou Dynasty led into the Qin Dynasty (221 - 207 BCE), small seal characters gained popularity. It is here that various scripts began to be adopted by different parts of the Chinese empire. It is also here where, along with the country's unification, the Qin Dynasty's first emperor simplified and unified the written Chinese language. Many of the characters that were seen during this period had a large influence on the standardization of the current Chinese characters.

Official script was then developed during the Han Dynasty (206 BCE - 220 CE). The integration of brush strokes and curves in character writing gained momentum during this time period, symbolizing the shift of Chinese characters into the characters that we make use of today.

Regular script was developed as a by-product of official script, becoming apparent in the southern and northern dynasties (420 - 589 CE). Stylistically, there were alterations made, opening the doors to the artform known today as calligraphy. It is from this point that the mainstream script was developed, with there being no major alterations occurring. Cursive writing appeared right after regular script, with individuals finding a more rapid way to draw Chinese characters. The disadvantage of this form of writing is that if one is not trained in reading combined strokes, there is little to no chance that the total meaning will be able to be fully understood.

China started to realize that the characters used started to become too complicated, leading to a drastic drop in literacy levels in the 1950s. It was during this time that the Chinese government decided to introduce simplified characters to aid in the learning and understanding of the Chinese writing system. What many forget is that there are thousands of characters that need to be practiced and memorized if one wants to master the written language. However, although a simplified character system was adopted by mainland China, Malaysia, and Singapore, Taiwan and Hong Kong have chosen to continue with the use of the traditional characters.

Wanting to provide those who are not native to China with the opportunity to learn the language, romanization was introduced. Students have the ability to utilize the Western alphabet to represent the sounds that are spoken in Mandarin. For those just starting out, this is the typical first step, as it allows there to be a bridge between the studying of Chinese characters and learning the spoken language.

The system that is adopted with teaching materials is Pinyin. With Pinyin superseding older romanization systems, especially zhuyin, it was adopted as the standard method of romanization in 1982. This set off a wide rally of acceptance as the United Nations followed suite in 1986. Singapore, the Library of Congress of the United States, as well as the American Library Association, have adopted pinyin as the most modern method of romanization.

When referring to the spelling of Chinese geographical and personal names, pinyin has made the process that much easier. Pinyin has established a bridging whereby translation from Mandarin to English is easier than before, further being utilized as one of the main methods by which Mandarin is being input into computers. The learning of pinyin has become mandatory across all Mandarin-speaking countries. Where there is more than one language being spoken as an official language, as is the case in Taiwan, irrespective of which language the child grows up learning, he/she will be taught Mandarin in elementary school.

The development of pinyin has increased the rate at which non-Chinese individuals are able to learn Mandarin. Pinyin has made it that much easier to self-study the language, allowing formerly illiterate individuals a better chance at integrating themselves into areas where Mandarin is the main language that's spoken.

Coupled with Chinese characters, pinyin has enabled many foreigners to learn the pronunciation of Mandarin whilst also explaining both the grammatical and spoken domains of the language. However, when we look into the pinyin usage in Taiwan, a country that purely uses traditional Chinese characters, a modified pinyin system called Tongyong Pinyin was created. Today, when visiting Taiwan, one will see the spelling of roads and stores in Tongyong Pinyin.

Although many, especially those from the older generations, were against the adoption of Tongyong Pinyin, the Taiwanese government created a system where legally, a Taiwanese citizen can choose which form of romanization they want on their legal documents. For example, when applying for a new passport, the personal names could be written in Wade-Giles, Tongyong, or Hoklo of Hakka.

Chapter 2:

Where Can Mandarin Be Used?

Mandarin has been growing in popularity, with five countries listing it as an official language. These countries all have more than 50% of their population speaking Mandarin, clocking in at approximately 1.3 billion individuals speaking the language worldwide. The countries that make up this number are China, Taiwan, Hong Kong, Singapore, and Macao. With that being said, there are 19 other countries where Mandarin has been adopted, though this is to a lesser extent.

A lot of people find that learning Mandarin opens many doors for them, especially in terms of career options. Translators and even educators are very popular jobs, especially in countries where Mandarin is an official language. The reason these jobs are well sought after is primarily due to the language barrier that prevents residents of Mandarin-speaking countries from interacting with other countries where Mandarin is not an official language.

Not only does this promote greater communication and development across various countries, but it allows for heightened degrees of innovation as Chinese individuals will now be able to participate on global platforms without fearing that having learned Mandarin will be to their detriment. Contrary to that, learning Mandarin further increases the degree of innovation a person or company experiences as the pool of applicants from which one can choose rises dramatically.

Education opportunities increase even more once one invests the time and effort into learning Mandarin. These opportunities cover both in-school and external schooling, where an exchange becomes possible. Many students, especially in the United States of America, do a school exchange where they visit China and participate in intensive language classes in an attempt to get into a better education system.

With China near the top of the worldwide rankings in terms of their quality of education, finding an avenue to enter into their schooling system should not be disregarded. There is an increasingly popular trend that international students are following that is choosing China as an area to continue studies.

China is the fourth most popular destination for travel, having the third -largest population of international students. This number falls very closely behind those of the US and UK. However, the trend that has been noticed the most is an increase in 10% per year across the past decade, making China one of the most popular study-abroad destinations in the world. When we compare this data to that of ten years ago, when a third of all China's international students were from South Korea, the level of diversity that is currently present is astronomical.

South Korea's contribution to the international student populace in China has dropped to 17%, primarily due to the options and reputations of Chinese universities now reaching further across the world. As of 2019, there were more than 20,000 students present across 13 cities in China, while in the past, most of the students were studying in Beijing or Shanghai. Other popular cities where international students prefer to study include Guangdong in the south of China and Liaoning in the northern area of Beijing.

Previously, there used to be a very large monetary implication for students who have wanted to study in China. However, China focuses on recruiting the most talented, providing them with state-of-the-art equipment and teaching facilities in order for them to really make a difference. The Chinese government has therefore invested heavily in establishing a financial support model that attracts international students. With more than 277 institutions providing over 40,000 scholarships, it should not come as a surprise that international students are flocking toward the opportunities that China is offering.

In 2015, approximately 40% of all international students were on a scholarship that was offered by the Chinese government. When we compare this data to that of 2006, there has been more than a 5-fold increase in the amount of scholarships offered. Typically, the government will provide both language classes and education in order to ensure that the international student is well equipped for learning and is effectively able to positively contribute to society.

Mandarin is further used in many streams of entertainment, which are starting to be readily adopted internationally. Given the current worldwide climate, there has been an increased uptake in not only listening to music that is in another language, but also watching television shows that provide subtitles. The globalization of the Chinese entertainment network has only proven to be of benefit to the populace as it has created an alternative revenue stream for the country.

Along with Mandarin, other languages that have started to become globalized include Japanese and Korean. For each of these three languages, there is a specific theme that has resulted in their worldwide adoption. For Korea, it was the introduction and uptake of Korean pop music (called K-Pop), and for Japan, the use of anime resulted in a sharp increase in individuals wanting to learn Japanese. However, for Mandarin, it was a smorgasbord of reasons. A few of these reasons include the following:

- The ability to establish friendships with a wide array of individuals from different cultural backgrounds. When learning Mandarin, you are not only allowing yourself to interact with those who are indigenous to Chinese speaking countries, but you are creating a sense of common ground for interaction with other international students who have also started to learn Mandarin. What many have done in order to strengthen the aptitude of their Mandarin language is look for a cross-language penpal. What you do is teach someone from China your indigenous language whilst they teach you theirs. They say that one of the best ways to learn a language is to converse with a local, and this is a mutually beneficial way to do just that.

- Many find that the language barrier present in other countries prevents them from visiting them. This is definitely the case in countries that have Mandarin as their official language. Therefore, it is human nature to want to overcome challenges that present themselves. This is why many take it upon themselves to learn Mandarin before either traveling or moving abroad. Not only does it make the entire experience easier, but it allows you more time to explore and delve even deeper into that country's culture (and this is time that would have been spent trying to figure out where to go next).

- Interest in Chinese drama shows has increased over the years. According to SHINE News, these Chinese drama shows (shortened to C-drama) have attracted so much popularity that they are now being streamed from Netflix, Hulu, and Amazon Prime. The show called *The Untamed* became a worldwide sensation, as there were people streaming from more than 200 countries, breaking all records within the Chinese drama industry. This has resulted in an increase in both professionalization and industrialization in the Chinese entertainment industry so as to cater to the growing international market.

Mandarin-speaking countries have always shown a need for international individuals to teach English within their schools and universities. The reason for this is to promote ease of communication with other countries. After all, English is seen as the standardized language of communication worldwide.

With that being said, many individuals obtain a basic bachelor's degree at a local university, then emigrate to a Mandarin-speaking country as an English teacher. While the salaries may seem rather small, one needs to take into consideration the very low standard of living in countries like China. This means that an individual will definitely be getting more bang for their buck.

To give you a little more insight, here are some of the expected earnings along with added benefits that one can expect when teaching English in China:

- Public schools: Salaries range from RMB 6,200 - 15,300 ($900 - $2,200). The benefits that come with this include working shorter hours in comparison to private schools, as well as having longer paid vacations. Most schools will offer teachers an option for free meals, which can be seen as a fantastic way to experience another country's food culture while saving money in the process.

- Private language academies: One can expect to earn RMB 6,200 - 16,000 ($900 - $2,300) per month. How this typically differs from public schools is that the salary earned is based on the amount of personal teaching experience you have, as well as the level of education that you have achieved. The curriculum at private academies tend to be more rigid than public schools, meaning that you will need to know a specific level of Mandarin in order to work at these institutions.

- Universities: In these pristine institutions, one can expect a salary of RMB 7,000 - 9,700 ($1,000 - $1,400). Along with this, typically there is a lighter workload and far fewer teaching hours when compared to other instructors. On top of the latter, those who teach English at universities also enjoy paid accommodation, free airfare, and more time to explore.

- International schools: These are where you want to teach as you will find the highest salaries. Expected salaries are RMB 11,800 - 29,000 ($1,700 - 4,300). However, landing one of these jobs is not only a lot more difficult, but there are sizably lower benefits and longer working hours.

Learning Mandarin before taking up a teaching position will enable you to adequately discuss the terms and conditions of your contract, as well as the benefits that come with it. You will also be able to establish relationships with your colleagues, providing a more comfortable working environment. Working abroad can make one feel rather alone, especially if you don't know anybody. Thus, being able to establish these relationships will also be beneficial for one's mental health.

Mandarin can be used to better understand your immediate environment as well. Whether you are in Singapore, mainland China, or Taiwan, it is likely that newspapers, news channels, and road signs will be in Mandarin. Thus, learning the language will result in fewer struggles as you begin to navigate your everyday life. The *Northwest Asian Weekly* has expressed the need for foreigners to actively read their country's respective newspapers. Not only does this create an understanding of current events, but it further allows one to develop an open and critical mind. Therefore, they recommend that one takes at least twelve months of intensive Mandarin classes before emigrating.

Obtaining adequate and correct healthcare also requires a small amount of language knowledge. Although most healthcare professionals are trained to converse with patients in both English and Mandarin, seeking and obtaining healthcare may prove to be very difficult if one cannot understand road signs or instructions indicating where to go.

Furthermore, many healthcare institutions only provide directions for how to take medications in Mandarin. Not understanding their diagnosis and the type of medication that is being given is worrisome and stress-inducing. *Psychology Today* has recorded that there is a 92% chance that an individual will default their treatment should they not understand how or why they are taking specific medication. Thus, in order to mitigate the chances of this occurring, a basic understanding of the Mandarin language should be obtained.

Mandarin is also used in promoting and reinforcing a form of cultural heritage among communities. With many different cultural events and festivals being based on historical teachings, the base tabloids that are kept in museums have more than likely been translated into traditional Chinese characters. Thus, in order to effectively understand the core of these cultural traditions and festivities, Mandarin needs to be understood. This means that by promoting a culture that focuses on learning Mandarin, the heart of specific cultures remains preserved.

A few examples of Chinese festivals and heritage days that have been preserved since before the Shang Dynasty which are still celebrated today include the following:

- **Tomb Sweeping Day: A part of the Qingming (清明) festival, this day has been celebrated for more than 2,500 years. This is when people will show respect to their ancestors by cleaning their graves, offering food or wine, and burning incense. At these tombs, they also pray for their families and that their ancestors will continue to watch over them, keeping them safe and healthy.**

- Dragon Boat Festival: Also known as the Duānwǔ Jié (端午节) Festival, it is a day of cultural prayer and worship honoring Qu Yuan, an exiled official who drowned in the Miluo River and whose body has never been recovered. Thus, every fifth day of the fifth lunar month, boats will be paddled out on a river to the sound of beating drums. This is with the main intent to keep fish and evil spirits away from Qu Yuan's body.

- Lantern Festival: Also known as Yuánxiāojié (元宵节), the Lantern Festival is a tradition that ends the Spring Festival (more specifically the Chinese New Year). For the past 2,000 years, lanterns have been lit as a way for people to pray for their futures. For example, women who would want to fall pregnant walk under a lantern that has the symbol of "baby" on it.

The Mandarin language has become ingrained in the societies of many countries, and learning the language has become necessary to navigate life within specific countries. However, it needs to be acknowledged that learning Mandarin is an ongoing process, requiring hours of dedicated studying and repetition. The amount of opportunities that learning Mandarin grants you with, however, knows no bounds and will only aid in your personal development.

Chapter 3:

How to Approach Learning Mandarin – Studying Tips and Tricks

At this point, you have already heard that learning Mandarin can be rather difficult. However, it is not knowing where to start learning that typically stops people from pursuing learning the language. One really needs to be sure that they are learning Mandarin for the right reasons, as passion fuels action; where there is no passion, there will be no action. Learning Mandarin is not for everyone, especially as it takes countless more hours to learn in comparison to other languages.

What is recommended is taking a free online class with either "Tutor Mandarin" or "eChinese Learning" to see if pursuing learning the language is right for you. Not only will you get a first-hand look at what learning it looks like, but you will get a feel as to how much time you will need to dedicate in order to truly learn the language.

Whether it be a personal goal or a rather impulsive want, it is advised to do some research on Mandarin learning materials that are available online. When it comes to learning the language, it is going to take a lot more than attending a few classes. Keats School and StudyCLI are two institutions that offer seminars, immersion programs and study abroad opportunities, which is perfect for anyone who wants to take their learning to the next level.

A resource that many recommend is called Fluenz. It allows you to consolidate the knowledge you have learned in online classes with the information that you are going to find in these two workbooks. The book that you are currently reading, as well as its associated counterpart, work perfectly with Fluenz, especially seeing as the amount of practice provided will have you reading and writing Mandarin in no time.

Make sure that you have a few notepads handy that you have dedicated solely to practicing your Chinese characters and pinyin. Preferably, try to pick a notebook that has large line spaces and margins as this will make jotting down characters that much easier while also providing more than enough space to practice the writing of the characters.

Learning pinyin will be the next step since it allows you to come to terms with how Mandarin words are pronounced and expressed using Chinese characters. With pinyin being the most commonly used system to learn written Chinese, it acts as a great introduction to the "one syllable" rule. This rule focuses on each Chinese character representing one syllable, which can be written out phonetically in pinyin. An example would be "wǒ shì zhōngguó rén" which has five syllables.

Thus, it is represented by five Chinese characters as 我是中国人. However, as you start to delve deeper into your studies, you will begin to realize that the pronunciation of pinyin is not as if you would read the word in English. An example of this is "shi", which is not pronounced as "she" but rather as "sure".

Once you have worked through the basics in this book and have a rather detailed notebook with all that you have learned, it is time to start speaking Mandarin to others. You will hear many saying that the best way to learn a language is to speak to a native speaker, and this is 100% true. With native speakers, they will be able to correct you regarding your pronunciation, allowing you to conceptualize where you are not pronouncing words correctly and rectify it before it becomes habitual. Conversing with a native speaker will also develop your confidence, allowing you to take your next step, which is constructing phrases from saying simple words.

You want to ensure that you are immersing yourself in the Mandarin language as often as possible, which is why listening to it during your morning commute is highly recommended. By doing so, you will begin to recognize sounds that go together and understand meaning in conversational Mandarin.

At the beginning, you may feel like they are speaking too fast, especially when you are listening to a news channel. However, you don't necessarily need to listen to the news; you could listen to a Mandarin podcast that teaches you a new Chinese character each day. This is why it is recommended to use "ChinesePod" to really maximize your learning. This becomes important when we start to look at the tones in Mandarin later on.

Many want the quickest route to learning Mandarin. This is why we decided to give you some studying tips and tricks to make your learning journey that much more exciting and fun. It is important that you are able to set both short-term and long-term goals, as this allows you to work toward something. For example, where do you want to be in terms of Mandarin fluency in three months, nine months, and one year? It is important to be realistic about these goals and base them off of how much time you are able to commit per week to learning Mandarin. As you move from your long-term goals to your short-term ones, set monthly goals that could vary from having memorized a hundred Chinese characters to even reading an easy Chinese book.

Also, make sure that these goals envelop the SMART criteria. This means the following:

- Specific (S): One wants to ensure that the goal that you have in mind is specific. Ask questions like, "What needs to be accomplished?", and, "What steps need to be taken to achieve this?" As you start to answer these questions, you are providing prompts that will ultimately establish a highly specific goal that is context-specific.
- Measurable (M): Adding numbers to your goal quantifies it, allowing it to be even more impactful. How many Chinese

characters do you want to have memorized in two months? 30? 100? Being able to establish these small yet concise goals provides a newfound self-confidence that establishes a positive growth pattern as you continue to learn Mandarin.

- Attainable (A): When a goal is reached, it should empower you to take the next step, which is why you need to have a serious reality check. Is your goal realistic? One cannot expect to have a hundred Chinese characters memorized in one month when only one hour per week is spent actively studying.

- Relevant (R): The best goals have a benefit attached when achieving them. You want to really delve deep and establish why this goal is important to you. Will learning Mandarin give you improved education prospects? Will it allow you to create a better life for you or your family? As soon as you attach a benefit to your goal, you make it more real, with there being a tangible result that you can gain once completing it.

- Time-bound (T): If you don't have a deadline imposed on your goals, you are going to keep procrastinating and, in the end, not reaching them. This aspect of SMART provides deadlines for your goals. Your goals can also have mini checkpoints that are time-bound. For example, if you want to learn a hundred new Chinese characters per month, this means that you need to learn twenty-five new Chinese characters per week.

Reviewing your goals and ensuring that they remain SMART is the key to not only achieving your goals, but learning Mandarin at a pace that fits your routine and schedule. It is important that you are not afraid to alter your goals. It is better to be realistic about your capabilities— given all your other commitments—than needing to deal with the emotional turmoil of not achieving your goals at all. This is where you need to create a learning plan and study timetable to ensure that you do not fall behind.

It is vital that you do not only dedicate one time period a week to learn Mandarin, but instead make sure that there is a set time every day that you study. Not only will this result in you learning the content more quickly, but it will ensure that your foundation is strong. It is advised to focus on short sessions of study, as our brains work best in small spurts rather than long and ongoing study sessions.

By incorporating activities that combine speaking, writing, reading, and listening into your daily schedule, you will learn Mandarin at a faster pace. As you want to combine these skills, there are definite ways that they can be practiced. A few examples are as follows:

- Reading and speaking: The easiest and most cost-effective way to combine these two skills is by reading aloud. As you continue to do this, you will realize the importance of tones, as well as ensure that you acknowledge them in speech. This will also help you in hearing how you will sound when you talk to others. Many find it helpful to make flashcards that they use to practice when they are commuting or when they are in a line at the grocery store. Some find that it is useful to match the content of the flashcards to the activity that they are doing. For example, learning some breakfast foods while eating breakfast or some work-related terms when you are in the office are fantastic ways to provide context to what you are learning.

- Listening and writing: What many find to be of great use is listening to any Mandarin-speaking show on YouTube, and then having a friend who is fluent check if what you heard was correct or not. Not only does this increase your capacity to listen intently, but it also allows you to become accustomed to the speed at which conversational Mandarin occurs. Doing this for approximately 15 minutes per day is highly recommended.

- Reading and writing: Typically, people just starting their Mandarin studies will find this aspect rather mundane at first. However, it really is the best method to master those rather difficult Chinese characters. You will begin to notice that there are many characters that look similar, with very subtle differences providing an entirely different meaning. An easy way to practise this is to read a sentence and then write it down. If you are a beginner, start off by writing the pinyin first followed by the corresponding Chinese characters below.

It is important that when you start learning Mandarin, even at the beginning phases, that you start to focus on phrases instead of the intricate nuances of individual vocabulary. Vocabulary is a crucial part to any language; however, one needs to ensure that there is context for the vocabulary to actually make sense. Try adding a phrase or sentence that uses a character that you have just learned. This ensures that you learn context, making it that much easier to use the content when having a conversation.

Remember, do not be daunted by the intricacies of Mandarin grammar. It is one of the last aspects that those learning Mandarin truly master, primarily because it comes with time. When learning them, make sure you fully understand one aspect before adding another. Otherwise, you will become confused by the very fine nuances and get frustrated.

If you find yourself to be a visual learner, we recommend the sticky note method of learning Chinese characters. Purchase a pack of different-colored sticky notes, letting each one represent a different category of words. Writing down characters and phrases onto these sticky notes and then putting them up on your wall will allow you to visualize the content more readily.

Furthermore, many find that putting the sticky notes on a wall near their door helps a lot. The reason for this is that they challenge themselves to learn or repeat a new Chinese character before they enter and exit the room. Thus, they are constantly interacting with the content, inadvertently including it as a part of their daily routine. If you cannot get a hold of colorful sticky notes, the same aspect can be applied using white one and an array of colorful pens.

Once you feel that you have started to get a grasp on the language, it is time to take the next big step. We call this "total immersion". What this encompasses is changing the language settings on your electronic devices to Mandarin so that you can learn to navigate the language in a hands -on manner. With this manner of learning, there can be both bouts of frustration as you cannot get where you need to go on your device and happiness as you successfully navigate your device. However, one needs to be sure that they are ready to undergo total immersion, because if not, it could result in an individual feeling intensely overwhelmed, to the point that one does not want to learn Mandarin anymore.

As you progress through your journey of learning Mandarin, you may find that the above tips and tricks may not necessarily work for you. However, that is the joy of learning a new language as you start to find what manners of learning really work for you. We are at the part of the book where you will begin to learn more about the practicalities of Mandarin, how to read it, as well as what some of the more common word choices are when speaking to friends, co-workers, and family.

The time to delve into learning Mandarin is now, so get your notebooks and pens ready as you physically begin your journey of adding another language to your repertoire.

Chapter 4:

Mandarin Character Uniqueness

Over 955 million people speak Mandarin as their mother tongue, surpassing English to be the most commonly spoken mother tongue in the world. Being the only modern pictographic language, Mandarin was developed using images, resembling a game of Pictionary. Almost all of the Mandarin characters are derived from actual historical images and objects. Let's take a look at the word "shan" which means "mountain".

Its character is 山, which looks like three points of a mountain range. With that being said, complicated characters that have up to 17 brush strokes are usually created by an amalgamation of smaller characters that build up to the overall character's meaning.

Typically, each individual character that makes up a more complex character is called a radical. An example of this is the word "feeling", which has 情 as its character. Now this character is comprised of three different radicals, as follows:

- Heart: 忄
- Plentiful: 丰
- Moon: 月

As we see that the combination of the above makes up the 情 character, as soon as you change any of these radicals, the entire meaning of the character will change. For example, if you were to change the "heart" radical you would be able to make 请 which means "to ask", and 清 which means "clear". This is where you are able to see the degree of character uniqueness that Mandarin shows. This does not mean that there has been no Western influence in some of the words adopted by Mandarin. A few examples are as follows:

- Amoeba: Āmǐbā (阿米巴)
- Bacon: Péigēn (培根)
- Bagel: Bèiguǒ (贝果)
- Chocolate: Qiǎo kè lì (巧克力)
- Coffee: Kā fēi (咖啡)
- Cookie: Qǔqí (曲奇)
- Golf: Gāoěrfū (高尔夫)
- Massage: Mǎshājī (马杀鸡)
- Sofa: Shā fā (沙发)
- Tuna: Tūnnáyú (吞拿鱼)

Each syllable in pinyin has a corresponding Chinese character. Thus, whenever you find yourself adding more pinyin to a sentence, you can expect additional characters to be written. This is how the "regular script" was defined during the Wei to Jin period. With regular script being attributed to Zhong Yao near the end of the Han Dynasty, he is typically known as the father of regular script. Having discussed him in a previous chapter, what we did not mention is that the earliest surviving pieces of regular script were, in fact, handwritten notes by Zhong Yao.

Having aided the development into dominant modern-day Mandarin script, a typical character is drawn today by using semi-cursive stroke, along with pauses to end horizontal strokes and heavy tails on strokes that are written in the downward-right diagonal.

It is because the characters are so unique that the task of memorizing them can seem rather tedious. However, to effectively tackle this challenge, we suggest adopting an eight-week studying timetable that focuses on learning radicals first before diving even deeper into the learning of Mandarin phrases. Here are a few examples of the radicals that one would typically find to the left of the Chinese character:

Radical	Radical as a character	Pinyin	Meaning	Examples
亻	人	Rén	Person	- You: nǐ(你) - They: tā men (他们)
氵	水	Shuǐ	Water	- River: hé (河) - Wash: xǐ (洗)
日	日	Rì	Time or Day	- Time: shí (时) - Early: zǎo (早)
女	女	Nǚ	Female	- Good: hǎo (好) - Mom: mā ma (妈妈)
月	月	Yué	Moon	- Wear: fú (服) - Friend: péng yǒu (朋友)
𧾷	足	Zú	Foot	- Kick: tī (踢)

					- Run: pǎo (跑)
扌	手	Shǒu	Hand		- Push: tuī (推)
					- Pull: lā (拉)
讠	言	Yán	Language		- Talk: shuō huà (说话)
					- Language: yú yán (语言)
口	口	Kǒu	Mouth		- Sing: chàng (唱)
					- Drink: hé (喝)
子	子	Zǐ	Child		- Child: hǎi zi (孩子)
					- Diligent: zī (孜)

The above is not an exhaustive list as there are also radicals that are present in other areas of the Chinese character. However, so as to not overload your brain, we will leave them out for now. There are more than 200 radicals in Mandarin, which means that even by learning two radicals per week, you are going to be studying them for quite some time. But why not have a little bit more fun with them by grouping them together based on commonality?

Remember, deciding to study Mandarin is not a quick fix to your desire to become a linguist. It is going to take a good couple of months, and even years, until you have mastery over the language. Having mentioned the eight-week program, here is an example that utilizes learning one radical per week:

- Week 1: Using the radical 人, focus on establishing a concrete foundation in your basic greetings and the use of pronouns. As using the correct pronoun shows a heightened level of respect when conversing with native speakers, ensure that you have a good understanding of it.

- Week 2: The radical 子 focuses on education and family, which require an understanding of the Week 1 radical in order to fully grasp the concepts of the Chinese characters.

- Week 3: It is highly likely that you will need to interact with a host family or a native speaker of Mandarin. This is why the radical 宀 is important this week, especially as it includes characters relating to "house" and "family".

- Week 4: Learning about how to communicate your level of Mandarin language capability, even if it is not much, is a fantastic way to let others know to simplify thoughts so you can understand them better. This is why focusing on the radical 言 is so important as it caters for all Chinese characters that have to do with "language".

- Week 5: You will most likely find yourself lost in a country where Mandarin is a native language. This is primarily because the road signs will only be in Mandarin. With that being said, this week you will need to focus on the 阝 radical, especially seeing as it refers to all characters that have to do with "directions".

- Week 6: Needing to move around a city is imperative. However, in order to do that, one needs to know the 辶 radical. This radical covers everything that has to do with "motion" and "transport".

- Week 7: The radical 疒 needs to be studied, especially if one must seek medical help. Referring to all characters related to "illnesses", it forms a core component of successfully being able to navigate life in a Mandarin-speaking country.

- Week 8: Being able to express yourself as well as your concerns is important. This is why characters regarding "thoughts" and "feelings" should be focused on during this week. The radical that you should look for is 心.

One can think of a complex Mandarin character as a mathematics equation where the result is a character that has in-depth meaning. There are a bunch of resources available online that list the 200 radicals. Using the above method of practice, add and remove radicals to be studied that week as you see fit and based on your capabilities and available time.

What you further need to ensure is that you do not forget what you have learned in previous weeks, especially as some of the characters with specific radicals will begin to build on one another. This is why it is suggested to spend 30 to 45 minutes per day recapping what you have already learned, especially before you jump to the next week's content. Remember that adjusting your schedule does not mean that you are a failure but rather that you are cognizant of your own abilities and want to ensure that you fully understand the context of the content before moving on.

Chapter 5:

Tones

One thing that is imperative to your success in learning Mandarin is understanding the tonal aspects of the language. With many linguists believing that tones did not exist during the use of Old Chinese, they do play a vital component in differentiating the meaning of words. Tones exist when writing pinyin and need to be adhered to as missing a tone could change the entire context of a sentence. There are many ways to learn how to pronounce tones, but it is important that tones are learned and pronounced correctly in order to ensure the topic of a conversation is maintained.

There are four main tones in the Mandarin language. These are as follows:

- First tone: This tone is referred to as "ping" (平) and is typically pronounced at a level but higher pitch. Its accentuation on the letter in pinyin is ā.

- Second tone: When pronouncing this tone, start off at a lower pitch, rising to end at a slightly higher pitch. Referred to as "shang" (上), the accentuation on the letter in pinyin is á.

- Third tone: Probably one of the most difficult tones to master, this one will have you start at a neutral tone, dipping to a lower pitch and then rising back to where you initially started. It is seen as the "falling and rising" tone, referred to as "qu" (去). In pinyin, its accentuation is ǎ.

- Fourth tone: Starting from a pitch that is slightly higher than neutral, the spoken syllable moves strongly and quickly downward. Called "ru" (入), it is often compared to the forcefulness of reprimanding another person. Its pinyin accentuation is à.

To provide some context regarding how important tones are, below is a table where the pinyin uses the same lettering but has different tones:

Pinyin	Chinese character	Meaning
mā	媽/妈	Mother
má	麻	Hemp
mǎ	馬/马	Horse
mà	罵/骂	Scold

Learning tones is not going to be easy; it requires a lot of practice. You also need to allow time for your ear to become trained to hear the different tones. At the very beginning, you will start to hear and analyze every individual tone. However, as soon as there is a case where tones are juxtaposed one after another, it may be difficult to fully comprehend. Even though you can hear that there is a distinct difference, if asked to replicate or reproduce that specific tone, you will most likely not be able to do it. If you are able to cultivate a willingness to want to pronounce the different tones, no matter how difficult they may seem, then you are well on your way to mastering Mandarin.

Typically, especially when you have conversed quite a lot, there is the development of a "3 -second memory". However, even after prolonged exposure, it is said that the memory of tones will only last three seconds. This is why there needs to be constant repetition regarding the initials, tones, and finals. There are specific "tone pair drills" that can be performed, and they are especially useful for getting accustomed to the tones that are juxtaposed.

A step-by-step process by which tone combinations should be tackled first is written below. It list starts with the easiest at the top, leading to the most difficult at the bottom:

- Tone 1 - Tone 1
- Tone 4 - Tone 4
- Tone 2 - Tone 4
- Tone 2 - Tone 2
- Tone 4 - Tone 2
- Tone 1 - Tone 4
- Tone 2 - Tone 3
- Tone 3 - Tone 3: There is an important rule regarding the positioning of two tone 3s next to each other. When this happens, the written pinyin will remain the same. However, regarding speech, the first tone 3 should be changed to a tone 2.
- Tone 1 - Tone 3
- Tone 2 - Tone 1
- Tone 3 - Tone 4
- Tone 3 - Tone 1
- Tone 1 - Tone 2
- Tone 4 - Tone 1
- Tone 4 - Tone 3
- Tone 3 - Tone 2

There will be times where you make tons of mistakes. These mistakes will even occur when you start to show tonal success when making a deliberate effort. This is to be celebrated, as it shows that you are one step closer to learning Mandarin. However, at the beginning of your language journey, you will most likely only be able to identify tones of pinyin that you have become well acquainted with. You will know that you are starting to progress when you are able to identify and imitate a tone on a new word that you have yet to learn.

Chapter 6:

Pinyin Pronunciation

Delving deeper into pinyin pronunciation, it is important to understand what pinyin is composed of. Typically, it will have three components. These are the initial, tone, and final. All three of these components need to be present in order for a Chinese character to be successfully represented by it. Not only that, but depending on the selection of initials, tones, and finals, the Chinese characters will be different.

In Mandarin, initials are also referred to as starting sounds. Typically, these cannot stand alone and need to be augmented or followed by a semivowel or final. Do not stress if this is yet to make sense as we are still going to delve into each respective component of pinyin before piecing everything together.

Below, you will be able to find the most common initials used in pinyin, as well as how they should sound. By merging this table with an online resource that verbally sounds it out, you will be able to make sense of them quicker and easier. The table of starting sounds is as follows:

| b | Pronounced as in English, as in bed |
| pPronounced as in English, as in pen |
| mPronounced as in English, as in moon |

f	Pronounced as in English, as in fool
d	Pronounced as in English, as in dirt
t	Pronounced as in English, as in turn
n	Pronounced as in English, as in no
l	Pronounced as in English, as in land
g	Pronounced as in English, as in gun
k	Pronounced as in English, as in king
h	Pronounced as in English, as in hand
j	Pronounced as in English, as in jean
q	Pronounced as "ch", as in cheese or change
x	Pronounced as "sh", as in shout or shin

Initials do not necessarily have to be single words. In Mandarin, there are initials that are a little bit more difficult to pronounce and consist of two letters. With these initials not being pronounced as they would be in English, they require a bit more practice. The *zh*, *ch*, *sh*, and *r* sounds are pronounced with your tongue curled up and touching your palate while pronouncing the sound. *Zh*, *ch*, and *sh* are essentially the same sound and pronunciation as *z̧*, *c*, and *s* respectively except, in the latter, the tongue is not curled. These can be rather tricky, so ensure that you spend as much time as necessary in order to really perfect these pronunciations.

Although these can stand alone without the need of a semivowel or final, they are written with an "i" at the end whenever they stand alone, though the "i" is silent.

zh	Tongue curled up, sounds like "ch" in English but has a more solid sound like the "ds" in buds
ch	Tongue curled up, sounds like "ch" in English but has a sharper sound like the "ts" in cats
sh	Tongue curled up, sounds like "sh" in English, as in shape
r	Tongue curled up, pronounced as in English, as in ring
z	Pronounced as tz, with a soft t
c	Pronounced as ts, as in cats
s	Pronounced as in English, like sin

Semivowels are seen as pieces of literature that exist in between a vowel and a consonant. Two of the most prudent examples in the English language are "w" and "y". However, when referring to

Mandarin, there are some letters that can be used as either an initial, semivowel, or final. A few examples of these, as well as how they are pronounced, are as follows:

i	Pronounced as "ee", as in feel
u	Pronounced as "oo", as in fool
ü	Pronounced like the "ou" in you

However, seeing as semivowels can be present on their own (i.e., without an initial preceding it), they are able to be incorporated in normal Mandarin conversation. The only alteration is the manner by which the semivowels will be written. Seeing as the above semivowels can be used interchangeably as either initials or finals, there needs to be some way by which they are distinguished, especially when being used as a semivowel. Thus, the following changes are made when using a semivowel in isolation:

- When the semivowel "i" is used, it is written in pinyin as "yi".
- When the semivowel "u" is used, it is written in pinyin as "wu".
- When the semivowel "ü" is used, it is written in pinyin as "yu". What needs to be noted is that the umlaut falls away when the semivowel is used as a single entity.

Finals are the last part of pinyin that is necessary for it to be completely understood. Here, you will need to know that finals can be grouped with initials, augmented with a semivowel, or can stand on its own. The only exceptions to the rule where a final can stand on its own is with: ê, ei, and eng. Here are a few examples of finals that are able to stand alone.

a	Pronounced as "ah", as in ah!
o	Pronounced as "oe", as in toe
e	Pronounced as "uh", as in duh
ê	Pronounced as "eh", as in ten
ai	Pronounced as "ie", as in lie
ei	Pronounced as "ay", as in bay
ao	Pronounced as "ou", as in loud
ou	Pronounced as "oe", as in toe (same as the above "o")
an	Pronounced as "un", as in undo
en	Pronounced as "in", as in Finland
ang	Pronounced as "ung", as in sung

eng	Pronounced similarly to the above "en" but with the "ng" pronounced as in English, as in sing or fang
er	Pronounced as "ur", as in fur

The following table will provide some examples of finals that are grouped with initials or are appended with semivowels. Not only do these make unique sounds that need to be studied in detail, but they can often be confused with each other. This is why we recommend that you fully understand and have conceptualized one sound before moving on to the next.

Finals beginning with "i"			
	With initial	Without initial	
i+a	ia	ya	Pronounced as "ia" in media
i+ê	ie	ye	Pronounced as "ye" in yeah
i+ao	iao	yao	Pronounced as "yow" in yowl
i+ou	iou	you	Pronounced as "yo" in yo-yo
i+an	ian	yen	Pronounced like yen

i+en	in	yin	Pronounced as "een" in seen
i+ang	iang	yang	Pronounced like young
i+eng	ing	ying	Pronounced as "ing" in sing

Finals beginning with "u"

u+a	ua	wa	Pronounced like "wa" in was
u+o	uo	wo	Pronounced like "wo" in world
u+ai	uai	wai	Pronounced like why
u+ei	uei	wei	Pronounced like weigh
u+an	uan	wan	Pronounced like one
u+en	uen	wen	Pronounced as "win" in wince
u+ang	uang	wang	Pronounced like "wan" but with the "ng" sound at the end

u+eng	ong	weng	With initial, it is pronounced as "ong" in song, but without initials, the "w" sound is also pronounced
Finals beginning with "ü"			
ü+ê	üe/un	yüe/yue	Pronounced like u-ye
ü+an	üan/un	yüan/yuan	Pronounced like u-when
ü+en	ün/un	yün/yun	Pronounced u-win
ü+eng	iong	yong	Pronounced as "yon" in yonder with the "ng" sound at the end

In some Mandarin texts, you may find that the umlaut of the ü has been omitted. This is completely normal. Seeing as it can be rather confusing in terms of pronunciation when the umlaut remains in many pinyin words, due to the commonality in speech, it is removed when written after "j", "q", "x", and "y". You will never find the semivowel "u" after any of these four initials.

Chapter 7:

Mandarin Character Brush Strokes

With Mandarin, there is always order to everything that is done. With that being said, when you start to practice drawing Chinese characters, you will need to do it in a specific order.

In this chapter, that order is going to be tackled, as well as the names of the different strokes. It will be important to learn the names of the strokes, especially when using more advanced Mandarin resources in the future. The reason for this is that they will assume that you already have the knowledge of what the stroke looks like from your beginner level classes. This is why, for ease of understanding, under each stroke, an explanation and picture has been included.

Types of Mandarin Brush Strokes

One of the simplest strokes is referred to as "héng" (横), and it is also the Chinese character for "one". Yī (一) is the name of the character for the number one. How one would typically draw this stroke is by placing the point of your brush on the left hand side, moving it from left to right in one swift motion. If you want to focus on the calligraphy aspect of the stroke, you will see that there are very evident areas of being pushed down at either end of the stroke. A visual representation is as follows:

Another simple brush stroke, which is literally the héng stroke propped onto its side, is the "shù" (竖) brush stroke. It is a vertical line that is typically combined with the héng brush stroke. The result of this is the Chinese character for the number ten, also referred to as "shí" (十). It is in this case that we need to take into consideration the order of strokes.

First, the horizontal stroke will be drawn, followed by shù. A fun fact regarding this character is that it resembles the Roman numeral ten (X) if it were to be placed at an angle. It can therefore be deduced that there is a possibility that both evolved from counting in tens, with a cross-stroke representing the completion of the group. When we look at the calligraphy of this character, the same rules apply for the héng stroke. The shù stroke will have the brush or pen pushed down slightly at the top (i.e., the start), and at the end, will be lifted off. A visual representation is as follows:

There are two diagonal strokes that are present as a component of many more complex Chinese characters. These two strokes are piě (撇) and nà (捺). Tackling piě first (the blue brush stroke in the image below), it is one of the brush strokes that makes up the character for "person", known in Mandarin as rén (人). Calligraphically, piě will always start at the top right. It then moves at an angle, down toward the bottom-left where the brush or pen will leave the paper. A visual representation is as follows:

The diagonal nà (represented as the blue stroke in the image below) brush stroke may or may not start in the middle of another stroke. However, in this example, the nà stroke will start in the middle of the piě stroke. It is when the piě stroke is combined with the nà stroke that the rén character is completed. This stroke, calligraphically, will always start at the top left and then angle downward to the bottom-right. As it leaves the paper, an impression of the brush or pen is to be made. A visual representation of this brush stroke is as follows:

There are many simple strokes in Mandarin. Another one of them is seen as a little dot, and it is referred to as "diǎn" (点) in Mandarin.

However, although it is seen as a small dot, it is a lot more than a very simple and quick up and down motion. Calligraphically, the brush or pen will be dragged to the right in a very slight manner. It will then be lifted to mimic a dot. An example of how this dot looks on characters is seen in blue below, but it can also be seen in the number six, known as "liù" (六). Referring to the number six character below, the diǎn is above the héng stroke. Typically, the diǎn will be drawn first, followed by héng, then lastly by piě and nà. This can be visually represented as follows:

Kicking everything up a notch, the next brush stroke is tí (剔). It is best seen by looking at the character for "I", known as "wǒ" (我). This is comprised of two different characters, "shǒu" (手) which stands for hand, and "gē" (戈) which represents a spear. However, focusing on shǒu, one can see the tí stroke. It is calligraphically represented by an upward movement that darts toward the right-hand side, being completed with a pointed end. This character is visually represented as follows:

In Mandarin, there is a concept known as the "composite stroke". This term refers to two different movements of brush strokes that are joined together without lifting the brush or pen. The stroke we will be

focusing on is the heng gou (横钩) stroke. To see this stroke clearly,

we will refer to the Chinese character for "write", called "xiě" (写). The heng gou stroke, which is drawn below in blue, is composed of a horizontal héng stroke followed by the hook, referred to as gōu. To calligraphically explain this entire character, we will break it down into segments. Reading the character from the top, one can see a vertical stroke first drawn, followed by the heng gou. Below, one can see the pictograph of a bird, representing that of a magpie. This character is visually represented as follows:

As héng can be adapted to form shù, heng gou can be adapted to form shu gou (竖钩). The downward shù stroke is terminated by a flick in order to give the hook-like appearance of gou. A Chinese character that consists of a shu gou, is "shǒu" (手), which stands for "hand". Describing the character below, it represents the lines that cross over the palm of a hand. The order in which these strokes are drawn are from top to bottom, with the shu gou stroke being drawn last. Keep in mind that this character is also the radical for wǒ that was discussed previously. The shu gou can be visually represented in blue as follows:

The gou hook can be added to a curved stroke, referred to as "wan". This will then result in the stroke you see below, called "wan gou" (弯钩). Calligraphically, the wan gou starts off at the top left, creating a curve that is first round then becomes vertical. It then ends in a hook as it states in his name. The wang gou forms an integral part of "gǒu" (note the different accent on the "u"), which means "dog" (狗). This character can be visually represented as follows:

When we look at the "wǒ" (我) character (the character for "I"), it does not only consist of a "tī" (剔) stroke. On its other side, there is a stroke known as "xie gou" (斜钩). How this segment of the character is calligraphically represented is by starting at the top, angling the brush or pen in a way that is curved toward the right-hand side. At the end, a hook is present. This is created by the brush or pen being lifted from the paper quickly as the brush or pen moves to the right. This character, with its xie gou segment in blue, can be visually represented as follows:

In terms of how horizontal a brush stroke goes, it not only depends on where the stroke starts, but also whether you are adding a hook onto the end or not. When we look at the horizontal ping stroke, it can be combined with a hook in order to create "ping guo" (平钩). The ping guo is seen specifically in the Chinese character for "heart", referred to as "xīn" (心). This character has three dots and is very common, specifically as it gives the addition of "emotion" onto a character. Examples of words that have characters that will contain the "heart" radical are anger, sadness, and longing. Calligraphically, the ping guo will start at the top and move straight down, curving to the right and ending in a hook. This can be visually represented in blue as follows:

Many a time, individual strokes can be combined to create a character that looks like a box. Often, there are two strokes that are used to create a right-angled stroke. The sharp turn that you see in blue below is called "zhé". This is combined with the two strokes joined by the

sharp turn, with the result being "shu zhe" (竖折). This stroke tends to be drawn last, especially seeing as it needs to be justified in size based on the contents that exist within the box. Calligraphically, this stroke requires a very delicate hand. One needs to ensure that their technique can create a sharp turn that does not represent a curve. Effectively, one is able to visualize this stroke as a shù stroke that is followed by a héng stroke combined into a single action. The shu zhe can be seen in the

character "yī" (医), which means "to cure or heal". A visual representation of this character is as follows:

There is a very typical box-shaped character that is incorporated in the word "mouth" called "kǒu" (口) in Mandarin. The stroke that we will be referring to in the below picture (represented in blue) is "heng zhe" (横折). This specific stroke is created by making a horizontal stroke to the right, followed by a pause, then going downward. The latter creates a stroke that is similar to shù. The radical that refers to kǒu is used readily in situations where speech or eating is described. The heng zhe stroke can be visually depicted as follows:

Now that you have a concrete understanding of basic brush strokes, as well as how they can link together, it is time to take it one step further. It is possible that three or more brush strokes can be combined in a variety of ways. One of these very common combinations is the "shu wan gou" (竖弯钩) stroke. This stroke follows the sequence of shù and wan, ending with a hooked gōu. This stroke is apparent in the Chinese character for "also", referred to as "yě" (也). Calligraphically, this stroke is drawn by making a very short vertical line downward, curving to the right, and finishing with an upward flick. The latter represents the hook. The yě character is an important one to remember as it plays a part in the creation of characters for the personal pronouns "he" and "she". The shu wan gou stroke can be visually represented as follows:

Another very common combination of strokes is "pie dan" (撇点). This looks like a letter "V" that has been turned 90 degrees to the right. Calligraphically, it is a slanting stroke that begins at the top-right, meeting a center point then ending with a left slanting stroke. The pie dan stroke forms a part of the character "woman", known as "nǚ" (女). It is important to know the nǚ radical as it can have both negative and positive connotations. Negatively, it has been used in describing women as being jealous or angry, whereas on a more positive note this radical is also found in the characters for good and peace. The pie dan stroke can be visually represented in blue as follows:

The final example, where a series of strokes are combined together, is quite a complicated stroke. This stroke is called "shu zhe zhe gou" (竖折折钩). The key to understanding complex strokes it to break them down. When we break down shu zhe zhe gou, calligraphically, we will start with a shu stroke moving downward. This is then followed by two sharp turns (as indicated by zhe zhe), ending with a vertical hook.

This stroke is typically seen in the Chinese character "horse", represented by "mǎ" (马). The shu zhe zhe gou stroke can be visually represented, in blue, as follows:

The Eight Brush Stroke Rules

When studying Mandarin, it is important that emphasis is placed on learning the sequences and directions that strokes should be drawn in. Not only will this ensure that you are able to draw Chinese characters correctly, but it will also save you time as you will become well accustomed to the steps necessary to correctly draw a character. As we look at examples of the eight different rules, remain cognizant that the deeper blue is the start of the stroke, with the gradient reaching a light blue in the direction that the stroke is going in.

The rules regarding brush strokes, are as follows:

- Rule 1: When drawing horizontal strokes, it is important to do so as the first stroke in a character. The reason for this is that they will often form the top of a Chinese character. To obey this rule, you will need to draw the stroke horizontally across and, only from there, move down if the character requires it. In the example below of shí, you can see that the rule is applied and followed.

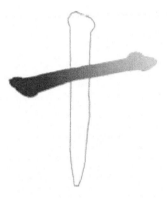

- Rule 2: If you are faced with a character that consists of both piě and nà, the strokes are to be drawn from left to right. What this means is that the piě will need to be drawn first before nà.

  An example showing how the left falling, then right falling rule is obeyed can be seen with the Chinese character for "person", known as "rén" (人). This is as follows:

- Rule 3: Characters are to be drawn from top to bottom. Historically, the reason for this was to prevent smudging of the characters when the numbers one, two, and three were drawn calligraphically. The number three has three horizontal strokes which are drawn from top to bottom. The Chinese translation of the number three is "sān" (三). This rule and character can be depicted as follows:

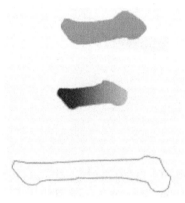

- Rule 4: Working from left to right, whilst following the previous brush stroke rules, is imperative in writing your Chinese characters correctly. With this being much easier for right-handed people, it may still take quite a bit of practice. A great example of working from left to right can be seen with the word "child", which is translated into Mandarin as "ér" (儿). This character, as well as the compliance to this rule, is depicted as follows:

- Rule 5: Always work from the outside to the inside. This is of paramount importance when you are writing characters that have an outside box as you will need to ensure that there is more than enough space for the inner characters. An example of where this rule is used is the word "together", translated to Mandarin as "tóng" (同). Remember that one will work from left to right, with the shù stroke (in brown) being drawn first, followed by the heng zhe gou stroke (in blue). This is diagrammatically depicted as follows:

- Rule 6: If the character has a completed box, the sealing stroke is done last. The reason for this is that it allows for the complete accommodation of all of the internal characters. Typically, the sealing stroke is a horizontal stroke that is drawn at the bottom of the character. The latter ensures that the rules already mentioned are being followed. To depict this, we will look at the word "country", translated into Madarin as "guó" (国). It is as follows:

- Rule 7: If you need to draw a character that has a central stroke that bisects the character, then it needs to be drawn before the left to right rule is applied. What this does is create symmetry for ease of reading and writing. An example of where this rule is applied is the word "small", translated to Mandarin as "xiǎo" (小). This central stroke is depicted, using xiǎo, as follows:

- Rule 8: A rule that is more focused on personal preference is the drawing of the character dots. Some people find it easier to draw the dots first as it provides them with a foundation for the construction of the rest of the character. Others find it easier to end with the dot. When we look at a rather common Chinese character, "de" (的), a possessive article, it seems that it would be simpler to draw the dot at the end. However, to reiterate, this is all based on personal preference. Here is a diagrammatic representation of where a dot can be situated:

Chapter 8:

What Can Go Wrong, and How

Can We Rectify It?

The world as we know it is becoming more interconnected. What this requires from us is the ability to adapt to these changes by learning different languages. Not only does learning a new language broaden our horizons, but it also increases our relationship circles as we have the capability to interact with a wider variety of people. When we learn another language, it requires effort, patience, and time. However, sometimes this is more difficult to achieve than we thought.

With that being said, we are going to tackle what could possibly go wrong while learning a new language, as well as what you can do to rectify these issues.

What Can Go Wrong?

Many times we remain transfixed in our errors that we tend to not be able to progress at the rate and pace that we would like. However, it is important to realize that you are not alone in this regard. It is common for individuals to feel stagnated when learning a new language, especially Mandarin. Before tackling what we can do to fix the problems, we need to first focus on what could go wrong.

Here are nine of the most common instances of what could go wrong, hindering your progress learning Mandarin. Take a look below.

1. Feeling discouraged by the mistakes that you make.

You need to remember that making mistakes is all part of the process. We can go even further to say that mistakes are important. Not only do they let you know where the gaps in your knowledge are, but they also create an additional learning opportunity for you to progress in Mandarin. As soon as you change your mindset so that mistakes are actually a fun part of the process, you will begin to see that the errors you are making are not as bad as they seem. It does not matter whether you are struggling with grammar, vocabulary, or character drawing— mistakes will happen. The quicker that you are able to deal with them, the better.

2. Not understanding the manner by which you learn.

How we decide to learn is just as important as the content that we are learning. One needs to understand what their learning style is, because the means by which we retain and interact with information is completely different. It is highly recommended that before you start studying Mandarin, you do a learning style test (there are many free ones online). Some of the questions they will ask may include, "Do you prefer reading about your interests over and above listening to them?", or, "Do you prefer a more hands-on approach when learning new concepts?" It is when you can understand yourself that you will be able to establish a tailored discipline toward learning and retaining what you learn during your journey.

3. Not starting off with the sounds.

One of the first concepts that one should focus on when learning a new language is sounds. With so many individuals not starting this way, they are already creating an unstable foundation, as well as more difficulty in learning Mandarin. You may feel the need to jump straight to reading and writing Mandarin, but how will you know if your pronunciation is correct without having studied the sounds? Verbal exercises are pivotal when learning Mandarin, especially because of the little nuances that are associated with the different tones in the language. By not starting with this first, you are already putting yourself at a disadvantage.

4. Your main focus is on the incorrect vocabulary.

One needs to be cognizant of the words that they are feeding their brain, especially at the beginning stages of learning a new language. Mandarin possesses such a wide variety of different categories, which can make it seem rather difficult when needing to choose which ones to focus on. When referring to Mandarin, learning the numbers, colors, vehicles, different types of food, and family members are good places to start. The words in these categories are simple enough to get you conversing with others, as well as diverse enough in order to ensure that you are practicing all the sounds necessary as a beginner.

5. Poor construction of sentence vocabulary.

Building sentences is a basic piece of learning another language, and it is frequently disregarded. There are a key amount of expressions that many beginners in Mandarin learn, especially if they want to travel to a country where Mandarin is the native language.

In English, a few of these expressions include the following: "Hi", "Farewell", "I apologize", and "Thank you". Learning these common expressions will help you grasp the context of Mandarin faster while also building confidence for when you speak to native speakers. If you do not focus on these important Mandarin expressions, you will most likely feel less confident in your speaking abilities. This will further result in you not being able to be corrected by others, ultimately slowing down the learning process.

When you start constructing basic sentences, it is important that you start to use simple verbs. Referring to these different verbs, there are numerous examples in the next chapter. It is when you begin to realize that the simple and basic sentences become easier that you can start to learn more complex phrases.

6. Fixating too much on grammar.

When you start learning Mandarin, it is important that you do not fixate too much on the grammar. It is when you start getting caught in the confusion of grammar that your focus shifts from learning the basics to wanting to become too good too fast. Grammar lessons will come later, and in terms of Mandarin, not learning it immediately will not hinder your progress in learning the language.

7. Worrying too much on pronunciation.

Remember that many who want to learn Mandarin wish to be perfect at it. It is when one becomes stagnated in wanting to be perfect in one's pronunciation, that progression is hindered. It can become extremely frustrating when you already speak a language that has its own tones. In this case, when you learn Mandarin, you might want to make the distinction in pronunciation as clear as possible. If you find yourself struggling with pronunciation, do not stress.

This is one of the first hurdles that you will need to overcome. The more that you practice a language, the more accustomed you will get to the unique sounds. Try your best to speak to native Mandarin speakers as much as possible, as they will be more than willing to point out errors in your pronunciation. It is important to understand that corrections in pronunciation are not a personal attack, but just natives who want you to succeed in learning Mandarin.

8. Listening to native speakers too soon.

One of the first tests to see how far you have progressed in learning Mandarin is to try your skills by speaking with a native speaker. However, if you start to speak to a native speaker too soon, there is a large chance that there will be a major drop in your morale if you do not succeed as well as you would have hoped to. Instead of only focusing on speaking, try intently listening to the native speakers talk. It is okay to not be able to understand what native speakers are saying. However, allow yourself the time to learn instead of feeling upset. Learning Mandarin is not a race; it is a journey.

9. Not being in the correct mindset.

We need to remember that we all live our own lives. On some days, we will be in the mood to learn Mandarin, and on other days, not so much. However, we cannot let one instance dictate our progress, especially when it comes to Mandarin. After all, it is a language that needs daily study, and if you are in the incorrect mindset for one day and do not study, you may throw yourself completely out of your routine. This may even result in giving up on learning Mandarin completely. What can be recommended is to give yourself a little pep talk when you do not feel like studying Mandarin that day. Reminding yourself of why you are studying Mandarin can also be a good method for shifting your mindset toward a more positive one.

What Can I Do to Fix It?

Sometimes you may feel hopeless as you have made an error that you just cannot fix. Unfortunately, these mistakes tend to happen more often than we think, especially when learning Mandarin. There will be times when you make either a vocabulary or even a stylistic error. Adults tend to feel embarrassed when they make a seemingly "silly" mistake. This degree of embarrassment knows no bounds, especially when they see children who are native speakers not making those errors.

When one makes a mistake, they tend to overthink absolutely everything. They even start to doubt their own abilities to learn Mandarin. It is when mistakes start to be made during the studying process that most Mandarin language students will choose to give up. A student who cannot speak out about their teachings will not progress, primarily due to the fear or judgment that is expected.

Psychologist Lev Vygotsky believed that those who succeed were those who failed the most. This is what you need to come to terms with as you study Mandarin. The biggest error you can make is not making any mistakes at all.

Previously, everything that could go wrong when studying Mandarin was listed. However, what can we do about it? Here are seven ways to embrace the mistakes that you learn as you study Mandarin:

1. Drop your ego.

If you have an ego, it is important that you come to terms with learning to let go of it. It really does not matter who you are. The fact is that you are on the same playing field as everyone else who is wanting to learn Mandarin. Thus, if you are the CEO of a successful company or still living in the basement of your parents, you are a person who is going to most likely make mistakes as you learn Mandarin. It is important that you start to integrate yourself into online groups with people who are at the same learning stage as you. This will heighten your accountability with each other, as well as provide you with others to practice your language skills with.

If you find yourself uncomfortable in conversation, lean on your emotions rather than your ego. Start by letting the other person know that you are still learning the language, and so to not speak fast. Start by smiling, apologizing, and then informing them that you are trying your best to study Mandarin and are fully aware that it's not perfect.

Refer to the workbook, where we will be discussing a few of the phrases that you can use. When you admit that you are not perfect, others will understand and appreciate the effort that you are making in learning their language, even if your language use is riddled with mistakes.

2. Try not to compare yourself to others.

One of the worst things you can do is compare yourself to someone else who speaks your target language better than you do. It is even worse when you find yourself comparing your progress to native speakers or advanced learners. By now, you know that Mandarin has a smorgasbord of nuances that make it an intricate and rather difficult language to master. This means that you are going to want to spend a lot of time on repetition, time which others may have more of. It is because everyone has different lives and lifestyles that their Mandarin language journeys will be different.

Some people are natural extroverts, so speaking comes more natural to them than with an introvert. Others may be good with listening. Some who start learning Mandarin may have a rather musical ear, meaning that the nuances regarding pronunciation can be picked up a lot easier, while others may find it difficult to really hear the subtle differences in the tones of Mandarin pronunciation. Some find it easier to study in groups online, and others prefer one-on-one lessons that are in person.

Each individual has their own unique journey that's based on not only their personalities, but also their current life circumstances. It is in this way that you should use your learning style to your advantage, making it the core of how you approach your Mandarin studies. Imitating another person's learning style will only provide you with ineffective study sessions, setting you even further back. However, do not completely cut yourself off from the study methods of others, as you could always learn something new.

Know yourself and what works for you, as well as what does not. Remember, you are not other people, and your life is not theirs to live. After all, there are those who would never envision learning another language, so you are already one step ahead!

3. Converse with yourself in your target language.

Self-confidence is imperative when learning a new language. Many will tell you that talking to yourself could be seen as rather weird, but in this case, it is a way to become even more comfortable with speaking Mandarin. It does not matter if you are washing your car, making dinner, or feeding the dogs—challenge yourself to speak to yourself within the context of the action that you are doing.

This is an even better way of overcoming a possible fear of speaking in public, especially if you have anxiety revolving around being embarrassed if you were to make a mistake. What is suggested to do in Mandarin is explore the pros and cons, as well as what your dreams, aspirations, fears, and concerns are. You will find that you are your own best listener. The monologues that you will end up having with yourself are fantastic ways to train, especially when one of your end goals is to be able to talk to people. The more often you talk to yourself, the more you will start to understand your own language imperfections, being able to rectify them as quickly as possible.

4. Learn from your mistakes.

In order for you to overcome any form of fear related to speaking Mandarin, you will need to understand the mistakes that you have made, as well as systematically work through each one.

In Mandarin, there are typically two cases in which mistakes will be made. These are listed below:

- You make mistakes because you do not know something.

- You make mistakes because you cannot remember something that you have previously learned.

If you were able to identify your mistakes as fitting the first case, then your solution is to identify what knowledge you are lacking, then learn it. The mistake that you're making could be a grammatical rule that you have yet to study, a word that you are unfamiliar with, or even the mispronunciation of a word's tone, altering the entire word's meaning. The latter is a very common occurrence for those who are learning Mandarin.

So how do you fix this issue? Well, you grab your textbook or dictionary. Studying with a teacher would also prove beneficial in this case as they can directly help you identify any gaps that you have in your knowledge, suggesting ways to fix them.

In the situation where you have forgotten concepts and/or words that you had known before, the solution is to continue practicing. Remember that when you find yourself erroneously using a specific tone, or you forget a word when it comes to using it, it does not have any representation of your intelligence level. The fact that you were able to identify a possible problem shows that you are cognizant about your own progress.

If you find yourself repetitively forgetting a specific word, write it down on a flashcard, and whenever you find yourself with some time to spare, go over all the words you keep forgetting.

5. Take it step by step.

It is always important to note that people who speak a language fluently did not wake up one morning and have the entire language and all the Mandarin characters memorized. They had to learn it, and it took time. It is important that you stop judging yourself so harshly, and instead, allow yourself to only be where you are meant to be.

An example of this is a beginner in Mandarin who is not used to making the tones of the new language. Do not expect yourself to have perfect pronunciation, as it takes improving a little each and every day to reach that level. As you move from the beginner phase of Mandarin to the intermediate phase, you will not make fewer mistakes, you will just make more complex ones.

You need to remind yourself that the next step will always encompass learning more and getting into a bit more detail. However, you need to find time within these steps to be proud of how far you have already come. One needs to learn to accept and revel in the little wins, especially once they complete one step and are ready to move on to the next one. This strengthens one's confidence as they begin to realize that they are capable of learning Mandarin.

6. Focus on your communication skills.

It does not matter whether you find yourself speaking to a friend, a co-worker, or a native speaker of Mandarin—focus on what you are trying to say at that moment. As soon as you allow your mind to drift, you will lose your train and thought, with the result being ineffective communication. It is important to always do your best so that you can remain confident in your capabilities. The task that you have when communicating is not to sound perfect when doing so, but rather to ensure that you get your message across.

Your sentence structure can be riddled with mistakes, but if you were successfully able to relay your thoughts, your objective has been met. It is at this point that you should celebrate, because you have taken one more step in becoming fluent in Mandarin.

Ensure that you are working on your communication skills in your own time. However, it is important that you do not let your mistakes hinder your progress of completing real tasks in Mandarin. You will find yourself in a cycle that consists of two parts: learn and apply. You will learn a new Mandarin phrase, apply it to a conversation that you are having, and then look for the next phrase to learn or build an already existing one.

7. Confide in yourself.

Your brain is an organ that should be marvelled, especially since it remembers stored information that you believe you had forgotten. Often, when we learn Mandarin, we get angry for not remembering one character. It is not the fact that we have forgotten all about it, but that it is just in that moment that we cannot remember it. This is when we need to allow our brains to take control, trusting ourselves in the process. Mandarin is not easy, but we forget that we have a brain that makes the seemingly impossible possible. You will find yourself feeling awestruck by its capabilities when you remember the word that you could not recall that morning whilst lying peacefully in your bed.

When you decide to put the effort and work into learning Mandarin, you will find that not only will you begin to trust yourself more, but you will start making fewer mistakes than you are used to. It is when we are in a stressed state that we freeze up, making errors that we would not typically make. This is why it is important to acknowledge your own abilities and how far you have come in already learning Mandarin. You must also trust the process.

A fear of making mistakes is what is going to be holding you back from perfecting your speaking skills. These fears need to be dealt with in a calm, collected, and healthy manner, or the repercussions could end up hindering your Mandarin progress even more.

Chapter 9:

Learning Some Words

By now, you have a strong foundation regarding how tones work, how to draw pinyin, as well as how to approach your Mandarin studies. Now it is time to apply some elbow grease as you start to learn some categories of Mandarin words.

Below, you will find some of the most commonly used terms that are most likely to come up in conversation. This is not an exhaustive list. However, if you find a word that is not in a category that it should be, write it in and start to create your own collection of Mandarin words.

Pronouns and Genders

Pronouns		
I, Me	我	Wǒ
You	你	Nǐ
You (formal)	您	Nín
Him, he	他	Tā

Her, she	她	Tā
It	它	Tā
Him, Her (godly/divine beings)	祂	Tā
It (animals)	牠	Tā
Plural pronoun		
Us	我们	Wǒmen
Them	他们	Tāmen
You guys	你们	Nǐmen
Possessive pronoun		
Mine	我的	Wǒ de
Ours	我们的	Wǒmen de
Yours	你的	Nǐ de

Yours (plural)	你们的	Nǐmen de
His	他的	Tā de
Hers	她的	Tā de
Theirs	他们的	Tāmen de
Its	它的	Tā de
Reflective pronouns		
Myself	我自己	Wǒ zìjǐ
Yourself	你自己	Nǐ zìjǐ
Himself	他自己	Tā zìjǐ
Herself	她自己	Tā zìjǐ
Itself	它自己	Tā zìjǐ
Genders		
Male	男	Nán

Female	女	Nǚ
Male animal	公	Gōng
Female animal	母	Mǔ

Greetings and Saying Farewell

Hello	你好	Nǐhǎo
Hello (formal)	您好	Nínhǎo
How are you?	你好吗？	Nǐhǎo ma
I am good	我很好	Wǒ hěnhǎo
Thank you	谢谢	Xièxiè
And you?	你呢	Nǐne?
How have you been?	你最近好吗？	Nǐ zuìjìn hǎo ma
Long time no see/it has been a while	好久不见	Hǎojiǔ bùjiàn (the bù is read as bú)
Good morning	早安	Zǎo ān
Good afternoon	午安	Wǔ ān

Good evening/good night	晚安	Wǎn'ān
Pleased to meet you	幸會 /高兴认识你	Xìng huì/ Gāoxìng rèn chí nǐ
Goodbye/see you again	再见	Zàijiàn
Let us meet soon	我们再约	Wǒmen zài yuē
I'm off/I'm leaving	我走了	Wǒ zǒule

Family Members

Mom	妈妈	Māmā
Mother	母亲	Mǔqīn
Dad	爸爸	Bàba
Father	父亲	Fùqīn
Husband	老公/丈夫	Lǎogōng/zhàngfū
Wife	老婆/妻子	Lǎopó/qīzi
Son	儿子	Érzi
Daughter	女儿	Nǚ'ér
Son-in-law	女婿	Nǚxù
Daughter-in-law	媳妇	Xífù
Child	孩子	Háizi

Older brother	哥哥	Gēgē
Younger brother	弟弟	Dìdì
Older sister	姊姊	Jiě jie
Younger sister	妹妹	Mèi mei
Grandfather (father's side)	爷爷	Yéyé
Grandfather (mother's side)	外公	Wàigōng
Grandmother (father's side)	奶奶	Nǎinai
Grandmother (mother's side)	外婆	Wàipó
Aunt (father's side)	姑姑	Gūgū
Uncle (father's brother-in-law)	姑丈	Gūzhàng
Aunt (mother's side)	阿姨	Āyí
Uncle (mother's brother-in-law)	姨丈	Yízhàng

Uncle (father's older brother)	伯伯	Bóbo
Aunt (father's older sister-in-law)	伯母	**Bómǔ**
Uncle (father's younger brother)	叔叔	Shūshu
Aunt (father's younger sister-in-law)	婶婶	Shěnshen
Uncle (mother's brother)	舅舅	Jiùjiu
Aunt (mother's sister-in-law)	舅妈	Jiùmā
Cousin (older male paternal cousin)	堂哥	Táng gē
Cousin (older female paternal cousin)	堂姐	Táng jiě
Cousin (younger male paternal cousin)	堂弟	Táng dì
Cousin (younger female paternal cousin)	堂妹	Táng mèi

Cousin (older male maternal cousin)	表哥	Biǎo gē
Cousin (older female maternal cousin)	表姐	Biǎo jiě
Cousin (younger male maternal cousin)	表弟	**Biǎo dì**
Cousin (younger female maternal cousin)	表妹	**Biǎo mèi**
Grandson (from son)	孙子	Sūnzi
Granddaughter (from son)	孙女	Sūnnǚ
Grandson (from daughter)	外孙	Wàisūn
Granddaughter (from daughter)	外孙女	Wàisūnnǚ
Nephew (from brother)	侄子	Zhízi
Nephew (from sister)	侄子	**Zhínǚ**

Niece (from brother)	外审	Wài shěn
Niece (from sister)	外审女	Wài shěn nǚ

Verbs

Accept	接受	Jiēshòu
Add	增加	Zēngjiā
Admire	欣赏	Xīnshǎng
Apologize	道歉	Dàoqiàn
Ask	问	Wèn
Become	成为	Chéngwéi
Believe	相信	Xiāngxìn
Bring	带	Dài
Borrow	借	Jiè
Buy	购买/买	Gòumǎi/mǎi
Change	更改	Gēnggǎi

Choose	选择	Xuǎnzé
Climb	爬	Pá
Complete	完成	Wánchéng
Cry	哭	Kū
Decide	决定	Juédìng
Deny	拒绝	Jùjué
Dream	梦想	Mèngxiǎng
Drink	喝	Hē
Drive (car)	开 (车)	Kāi (chē)
Eat	吃	Chī
Enjoy	享受	Xiǎngshòu
Examine	检查	Jiǎnchá
Explain	说明	Shuōmíng

Fall	摔倒	Shuāi dǎo
Feel	感觉	Gǎnjué
Fly	飞	Fēi
Forget	忘记	Wàngjì
Get	得到	Dédào
Give	给	Gěi
Hide	躲	Duǒ
Hit	打	Dǎ
Hug	拥抱	Yǒngbào
Introduce	介绍	Jièshào
Jog	慢跑	Mànpǎo
Joke	开玩笑	Kāiwánxiào
Jump	跳	Tiào

Kick	踢	Tī
Kiss	吻	Wěn
Laugh	笑	Xiào
Leave	离开	Líkāi
Look	看	Kàn
Meet	遇到	Yù dào
Need	需要	Xūyào
Open	打开	Dǎkāi
Pay	付	Fù
Practice	练习	Liànxí
Prepare	准备	**Zhǔnbèi**
Push	推	Tuī
Quit	放弃	Fàngqì

Read	读	Dú
Relax	放松	Fàngsōng
Remember	记得	Jìdé
Run	跑	**Pǎo**
Say	说	Shuō
Sell	卖	Mài
Sing	唱	Chàng
See	看	Kàn
Speak	说话	Shuōhuà
Stand	站	Zhàn
Study	读书	Dúshū
Take	拿	Ná
Think	想	**Xiǎng**

Try	试	Shì
Understand	理解	Lǐjiě
Wait	等待	Děngdài
Walk	走	Zǒu
Wash	洗	Xǐ
Write	写	Xiě

Numbers

Zero	零	Líng
One	一	Yī / Yāo

Yāo is mainly used when reading out phone numbers or sequence of numbers.

Two	二 / 兩	Èr/liǎng

Èr is used when saying 2 or 20, but from the hundreds upward, liǎng is used.

Èr is also used when referring to positioning, i.e., second place 第二名 (Dì èr míng).

Three	三	Sān
Four	四	Sì
Five	五	Wǔ
Six	六	Liù
Seven	七	Qī

Eight	八	Bā
Nine	九	Jiǔ
Ten	十	Shí
Eleven	十一	Shí yī
Twelve	十二	Shí èr
Twenty	二十	Èr shí
Twenty-one	二十一	Èr shí yī
Thirty	三十	Sān shí
Hundreds	百	Bǎi
One hundred	一百	Yībǎi
One hundred and five	一百零五	Yībǎi líng wǔ
One hundred and ten	一百一十	Yībǎi yīshí

One hundred and forty-three	一百四十三	Yībǎi sì shí sān
Two hundred	二百	Liǎng bǎi
Twohundredand twenty-two	兩百二十二	Liǎngbǎi Èrshí'èr
Two hundred and fifty six	兩百五十六	Liǎngbǎi Wǔshíliù
Thousands	千	Qiān
One thousand	一千	Yì qiān
Two thousand	兩千	Liǎng qiān
Ten thousand	万	Wàn
Hundred-thousand	十万	Shí wàn
Million	百万	Bǎi wàn
Hundred-million	亿	Yì

Trillion	兆	Zhào

Animals

Animals	动物	Dòngwù
Ant	蚂蚁	Mǎyǐ
Baboon	狒狒	Fèifèi
Bat	蝙蝠	Biānfú
Bear	熊	Xióng
Bee	蜜蜂	Mìfēng
Bird	鸟	Niǎo
Buffalo	水牛	Shuǐniú
Butterfly	蝴蝶	Húdié
Camel	骆驼	Luòtuó
Cat	猫	Māo

Caterpillar	毛毛虫	Máo máo chóng
Cheetah	猎豹	Lièbào
Chicken	鸡	Jī
Cow	牛	Niú
Crab	螃蟹	Pángxiè
Cricket	蟋蟀	Xīshuài
Crocodile	鳄鱼	Èyú
Deer	鹿	Lù
Dog	狗	Gǒu
Dolphin	海豚	Hǎitún
Donkey	驴	Lǘ
Dove	鸽子	Gēzi
Duck	鸭子	Yāzi

Eagle	老鹰	Lǎoyīng
Elephant	大象	Dàxiàng
Fish	鱼	Yú
Fly	苍蝇	Cāngyíng
Fox	狐狸	Húlí
Frog	青蛙	Qīngwā
Goat	山羊	Shānyáng
Hawk	老鹰	Lǎoyīng
Horse	马	**Mǎ**
Impala	黑斑羚	Hēi bān líng
Kangaroo	袋鼠	**Dàishǔ**
Leopard	豹	Bào
Lion	狮子	Shīzi

Lizard	蜥蜴	Xīyì
Lobster	龙虾	Lóngxiā
Monkey	猴子	Hóuzi
Mosquito	蚊子	Wénzi
Moth	蛾	É
Mouse	老鼠	Lǎoshǔ
Octopus	章鱼	Zhāngyú
Ostrich	鸵鸟	Tuóniǎo
Owl	猫头鹰	Māotóuyīng
Panda	熊猫	Xióngmāo
Peacock	孔雀	Kǒngquè
Penguin	企鹅	Qǐ'é
Pig	猪	Zhū

Pigeon	鸽子	Gēzi
Rabbit	兔子	**Tùzǐ**
Salmon	三文鱼	Sānwènyú
Shark	鲨鱼	Shāyú
Sheep	羊	Yáng
Snail	蜗牛	Wōniú
Spider	蜘蛛	Zhīzhū
Tiger	老虎	**Lǎohǔ**
Whale	鲸鱼	Jīngyú
Wolf	狼	Láng
Zebra	斑马	Bānmǎ

Body Parts

Head	头	Tóu
Face	脸	Liǎn
Eyebrow	眉	Méi
Eyes	眼睛	Yǎnjīng
Nose	鼻子	Bízi
Ears	耳朵	Ěrduǒ
Mouth	口	Kǒu
Teeth	牙齿	Yáchǐ
Tongue	舌	Shé
Nostrils	鼻孔	Bíkǒng
Hair	头发	Tóufà

Beard	胡子	Húzi
Neck	颈部	Jǐng bù
Throat	喉	Hóu
Shoulders	肩膀	Jiānbǎng
Arms	手臂	Shǒubì
Elbow	手肘	Shǒuzhǒu
Wrist	手腕	Shǒuwàn
Hand	手	Shǒu
Fingers	手指	Shǒuzhǐ
Nails	指甲	Zhǐjiǎ
Palm	手掌	Shǒuzhǎng
Chest	胸部	Xiōngbù

Abdomen	腹部	Fùbù
Hip	臀部	Túnbù
Waist	腰部	Yāobù
Legs	腿	Tuǐ
Thighs	大腿	Dàtuǐ
Calves	小腿	Xiǎotuǐ
Knee	膝盖	Xīgài
Ankle	脚踝	Jiǎohuái
Feet	脚	Jiǎo
Toes	脚趾	Jiǎozhǐ
Brain	脑	Nǎo
Lungs	肺	Fèi

Heart	心	Xīn
Stomach	胃	Wèi
Intestines	肠子	Cháng zi
Liver	肝	Gān
Kidneys	肾脏	Shènzàng
Bladder	膀胱	Pángguāng
Arteries	动脉	Dòng mài
Veins	静脉	Jìngmài

Plants and Nature

Tree	树	Shù
Leaf	叶	Yè
Branch	科	Kē
Trunk	树干	Shùgàn
Roots	树根	Shùgēn
Flower	花	Huā
Petal	花瓣	Huābàn
Thorn	刺	Cì
Grass	草	**Cǎo**
Rose	玫瑰	Méiguī
Orchid	兰花	Lánhuā

Chrysanthemum	菊花	Júhuā
Sunflower	向日葵	Xiàngrìkuí
Lavender	薰衣草	Xūnyīcǎo
Cactus	仙人掌	Xiānrénzhǎng
Moss	苔藓	**Táixiǎn**
Vines	葡萄藤	Pútáo téng
Ground	地	Dì
Soil	土	**Tǔ**
Water	水	**Shuǐ**
Air	空气	Kōngqì
Sun	太阳	Tàiyáng
Clouds	云	Yún
Sky	天空	Tiānkōng

Star	星星	Xīngxīng
Moon	月亮	Yuèliàng
Sea	海	Hǎi
Ocean	海洋	Hǎiyáng
Waves	波浪	Bōlàng
Beach	海滩	Hǎitān
Sand	砂	Shā
Stone	石头	Shítou
Rain	雨	Yǔ
Fog	雾气	Wùqì
Dew	露水	Lùshuǐ
Smoke	烟	Yān
Mountains	山脉	Shānmài

Hills	山丘	Shānqiū
Forest	森林	Sēnlín
Fire	火	**Huǒ**
Cave	洞穴	Dòngxué
Desert	沙漠	Shāmò

Fruits, Vegetables, Nuts, and Grains

Fruit	水果	Shuǐguǒ
Vegetables	蔬菜	Shūcài
Nuts	坚果	Jiānguǒ
Grains	谷类	Gǔlèi
Apple	苹果	Píngguǒ
Banana	香蕉	Xiāngjiāo
Lemon	柠檬	Níngméng
Mango	芒果	Mángguǒ
Kiwi	奇异果	Qíyì guǒ
Pear	梨	Lí
Apricot	杏子	Xìngzi

Avocado	鳄梨	È lí
Blueberry	蓝莓	Lánméi
Cherry	樱桃	Yīngtáo
Coconut	椰子	Yēzi
Grapes	葡萄	Pútáo
Guava	番石榴	Fān shíliú
Honeydew	蜜瓜	Mì guā
Lychee	荔枝	Lìzhī
Papaya	番木瓜	Fān mùguā
Passionfruit	百香果	Bǎixiāng guǒ
Peach	桃子	Táozi
Pineapple	菠萝	Bōluó
Plum	李子	Lǐzǐ

Pomegranate	石榴	Shíliú
Strawberry	草莓	Cǎoméi
Tomato	番茄	Fānqié
Watermelon	西瓜	Xīguā
Beetroot	红菜头	Hóng cài tóu
Bell pepper	灯笼椒	Dēnglóng jiāo
Broccoli	西兰花	Xī lánhuā
Cabbage	卷心菜	Juǎnxīncài
Carrots	萝卜	Luóbo
Cauliflower	菜花	Càihuā
Celery	芹菜	Qíncài
Chilli	辣椒	Làjiāo
Cucumber	黄瓜	Huángguā

Eggplant	茄子	Qiézi
Garlic	大蒜	Dàsuàn
Ginger	生姜	Shēngjiāng
Green peas	青豆	Qīngdòu
Kale	羽衣甘蓝	Yǔyī gānlán
Lettuce	生菜	Shēngcài
Mushrooms	蘑菇	Mógū
Olives	橄榄	**Gǎnlǎn**
Onion	洋葱	Yángcōng
Potato	土豆	**Tǔdòu**
Pumpkin	南瓜	Nánguā
Radish	萝卜	Luóbo
Spinach	菠菜	Bōcài

Spring onion	葱	Cōng
Sweet potato	红薯	Hóngshǔ
Sweetcorn	甜玉米	Tián yùmǐ
Turnip	芜菁	Wú jīng
Zucchini	夏南瓜	Xià nánguā
Almond	杏仁	Xìngrén
Barley	大麦	Dàmài
Cashew	腰果	Yāoguǒ
Chickpea	鹰嘴豆	Yīng zuǐ dòu
Lentils	扁豆	**Biǎndòu**
Macadamia	澳洲坚果	Àozhōu jiānguǒ
Oats	燕麦	Yànmài
Peanut	花生	Huāshēng

Pecan	胡桃	Hútáo
Rice	米	Mǐ
Soy	黄豆	Huángdòu
Walnut	核桃	Hétáo
Wheat	小麦	**Xiǎomài**

Food and Drink

Barbeque	烧烤	Shāokǎo
Bread	面包	Miànbāo
Burgers	汉堡	Hànbǎo
Burrito	墨西哥卷饼	Mòxīgē juǎn bǐng
Cheese	起司	Qǐ sī
French fries	薯条	Shǔ tiáo
Egg fried rice	咖喱	Gālí
Eggs	蛋炒饭	Dàn chǎofàn
Fried chicken	蛋	Dàn
Fries	炸鸡	Zhá jī
Hotdogs	热狗	Règǒu

Pasta	意大利面条	Yìdàlì miàn tiáo
Pies	派	Pài
Pizza	比萨	**Bǐsà**
Salad	沙拉	Shālā
Salt	盐	Yán
Sandwich	三明治	Sānmíngzhì
Soup	汤	Tāng
Steak	牛扒	Niú bā
Stir-fry	热炒	**Rè chǎo**
Sushi	寿司	Shòusī
Taco	塔科	Tǎ kē
Tofu	豆腐	Dòufu
Butter	牛油	Niú yóu

Cake	蛋糕	Dàngāo
Chocolate	巧克力	Qiǎokèlì
Cookies	饼干	Bǐnggān
Crackers	苏打饼干	Sūdǎ bǐnggān
Dessert	甜点	Tiándiǎn
Doughnuts	甜甜圈	Tián tián quān
Ice cream	冰淇淋	Bīngqílín
Pancakes	薄煎饼	Báo jiānbing
Peanut butter	花生酱	Huāshēngjiàng
Scones	司康饼	Sī kāng bǐng
Sugar	糖	Táng
Sweets	糖果	Tángguǒ
Waffles	威化饼	Wēi huà bǐng

Yogurt	酸奶	Suānnǎi
Beer	啤酒	Píjiǔ
Cocktail	鸡尾酒	Jīwěijiǔ
Coffee	咖啡	Kāfēi
Hot chocolate	热可可	Rè kěkě
Juice	果汁	Guǒzhī
Milkshake	奶昔	Nǎi xī
Soda	苏打	Sūdǎ
Tea	茶	Chá
Water	水	Shuǐ
Wine	葡萄酒	Pútáojiǔ

In the House and Around Our Daily Lives

House	房屋	Fángwū
Garden	花园	Huāyuán
Gate	铁门	Tiě mén
Door	门	Mén
Front yard	前院	Qián yuàn
Pool	游泳池	Yóuyǒngchí
Window	窗口	Chuāngkǒu
Stairs	楼梯	Lóutī
Garage	车库	Chēkù
Corridor	走廊	Zǒuláng
Carpet	地毯	Dìtǎn

Floor	地板	Dìbǎn
Roof	屋顶	Wūdǐng
Walls	墙	Qiáng
Living room	客厅	Kètīng
Sofa	沙发	Shāfā
Remote controller	遥控器	Yáokòng qì
Television	电视	Diànshì
Bedroom	卧室	Wòshì
Bed	床	Chuáng
Pillow	枕头	Zhěntou
Curtain	窗帘	Chuānglián
Beddings	床上用品	Chuángshàng yòngpǐn

Wardrobe	衣柜	Yīguì
Clothes	衣服	Yīfú
Shirt	衬衫	Chènshān
Pants	裤子	Kùzi
Shoes	鞋子	Xiézi
Makeup	化妆品	Huàzhuāngpǐn
Kitchen	厨房	Chúfáng
Cupboard	橱柜	Chúguì
Chair	椅子	Yǐzi
Table	桌子	Zhuōzi
Fridge	冰箱	Bīngxiāng
Stove	炉子	Lúzǐ
Sink	水槽	Shuǐcáo

Bathroom	浴室	Yùshì
Shower	淋浴	Línyù
Bathtub	浴缸	Yùgāng
Tap	水龙头	**Shuǐlóngtóu**
Mirror	镜子	Jìngzi
Clock	时钟	Shízhōng
Decoration	装饰	Zhuāngshì
Painting	画作	Huàzuò
Lights	灯	Dēng
Car	汽车	Qìchē
Keys	钥匙	Yàoshi
Motorbike	摩托车	Mótuō chē
Bicycle	自行车	Zìxíngchē

Aeroplane	飞机	Fēijī
Bus	巴士站	Bāshì
Train	火车站	Huǒchē
Ship	船	Chuán
Laptop	笔记本电脑	Bǐjìběn diànnǎo
Computer	电脑	Diànnǎo
Smartphone	手机	Shǒujī
Telephone	电话	Diànhuà
Watch	手表	Shǒubiǎo

Society

School	学校	Xuéxiào
Hospital	医院	Yīyuàn
Police station	警察局	**Jǐngchá jú**
Fire brigade	消防队	Xiāofáng duì
Government	政府	**Zhèngfǔ**
Shopping mall	购物中心	Gòu wù zhòng xīn
Church	教会	Jiàohuì
University	大学	Dàxué
Park	公园	Gōngyuán
Neighbours	邻居	Línjū
Office	办公室	Bàngōngshì

Doctors	医生	Yīshēng
Nurses	护士	Hùshì
Police	警察	**Jǐngchá**
Firefighters	消防员	Xiāofáng yuán
Clerks	文员	Wényuán
Teachers	老师	Lǎoshī
Students	学生	Xuéshēng

Common Words

This	这个	Zhège
That	那个	Nàge
These	这些	Zhèxiē
Those	那些	Nàxiē
Good	好	**Hǎo**
Bad	坏	Huài
Morning	早上	**Zǎoshàng**
Afternoon	下午	**Xiàwǔ**
Evening	晚上	**Wǎnshàng**
Breakfast	早餐	Zǎocān
Lunch	午餐	Wǔcān

Supper	晚餐	Wǎncān
North	北	Běi
East	东	Dōng
South	南	Nán
West	西	Xī
Left	左	Zuǒ
Right	右	Yòu
Up	上	Shàng
Down	下	Xià
Centre	中央	Zhōngyāng
Outside	外	Wài
Inside	内	Nèi
High	高	Gāo

Low	低	Dī
Big	大	Dà
Small	小	Xiǎo

Conclusion

Having reached the end of this book, we want you to give yourself a pat on the back! You started your journey to learn Mandarin, and to have come this far is no small feat. At this point, you should be well acquainted with the historical significance of the Mandarin language, as well as be familiar with where it can be utilized both in your personal life and beyond. You will also have hopefully established a newfound yearning to continue learning Mandarin. Remember, your journey doesn't end here; this is only the beginning.

You have learned the basics of Mandarin, extending from the various types of tones to being able to differentiate between many different pinyin and Chinese characters. Now that you have successfully conquered this first book, you should be well apt to learn all of the Mandarin words within it, and you should also be able to start constructing some short and concise sentences.

Here are some ways you can progress from your current level:

- Start to studiously work through the workbook that comes with this book. Not only will it aid you in fine-tuning your character writing skills, but it will also show you where there are gaps in your knowledge, as well as which rules need to be revisited to fill these gaps. This book should act as your own personal encyclopedia for when you need to review some basic concepts.

- Why not try the HSK test? The HSK is a fantastic method for testing how well your reading, writing, listening, and speech have progressed. It will show you how well you are progressing and provide you with some context of what level of Mandarin you need to achieve to not only converse with native speakers, but also to be considered fluent.

- Start to follow the steps as mentioned in the previous chapters about fully integrating yourself within Mandarin. Start to change your technological devices to the Mandarin language. Also, try your best to find a native speaker with whom you can practice your speech and listening skills and who will correct you when you make a mistake. The only way that you will really progress is by challenging your current level of knowledge.

It is important to remember that you need to consistently be reviewing and learning new words. Repetition is key if your end goal is to master Mandarin. Make sure you are confident in your current abilities before you traverse into a new category of information. In this book, we purposefully did not focus too much on grammar, as you need to have a strong foundation in understanding the nuances of the language first. Your next focus will be to incorporate what you currently know into your everyday life.

You took the step that many others were too scared to take. You remained determined, dedicated, and realistic in your goal-setting in order to reach the end of this book. Remember that this book should be seen as a reference to you. Do not beat yourself up when you erroneously use a tone that was not there. Instead, revisit the content in this book so that you do not make the same mistake again.

You have come this far and will continue to venture even further. Well done, and good luck on the road ahead. Never forget that you are capable of more than you think you are. You will continue to grow from strength to strength on your journey in learning Mandarin.

References

AllSet Learning. (2020, May 3). *Four tones.* Chinese Pronunciation Wiki. https://resources.allsetlearning.com/chinese/pronunciation/F our_tones

Ben, E. (2018, March 15). *10 common mistakes language learners make (and how to fix them).* Matador Network. https://matadornetwork.com/read/10-common-mistakes-language-learners-make-fix/

Boogaard, K. (2019, January 25). *An explanation of SMART goals and how to write them.* Work Life by Atlassian. https://www.atlassian.com/blog/productivity/how-to-write-smart-goals#:~:text=SMART%20is%20an%20acronym%20that

China Highlights. (2019a). *Dragon Boat Festival 2019.* China Highlights. https://www.chinahighlights.com/festivals/dragon-boat-festival.htm

China Highlights. (2019b). *Qingming Festival.* China Highlights. https://www.chinahighlights.com/festivals/qingming-festival.htm

Free Language. (n.d.). *9 Steps to Overcome the Fear of Speaking a Foreign Language | Free Language.* Freelanguage.org. Retrieved December 19, 2020, from https://freelanguage.org/how-to-learn-languages/9-steps-to-overcome-the-fear-of-speaking-a-foreign-language

Global Exam Blog. (2016, September 7). *100 million students learning Mandarin in 2020.* GlobalExam Blog. https://global-exam.com/blog/en/100-million-students-learning-mandarin-

in-
2020/#:~:text=The%20increase%20in%20students%20learnin
g

Huizhongmcmillen, A. (n.d.). *Easy as ABC: 8 Foolproof Tips for Learning
Chinese Faster.* Retrieved December 17, 2020, from
https://www.fluentu.com/blog/chinese/2016/01/18/tips-for-
learning-chinese/

I Will Teach You A Language. (2017, July 10). *7 Ways to Embrace
Mistakes When Speaking a Foreign Language.* I Will Teach You A
Language. https://iwillteachyoualanguage.com/blog/embrace-
mistakes

McCollum-Martinez, C. (2019, January 10). *What Salary Will You Earn
Teaching Abroad in China? | Go Overseas.* Www.Gooverseas.com.
https://www.gooverseas.com/blog/teaching-english-in-china-
salary

Minsky, C. (2016, September 12). *Five reasons why you should study in
China.* Times Higher Education (THE).
https://www.timeshighereducation.com/student/advice/five-
reasons-why-you-should-study-china

Pinyin Guide. (n.d.). *Pinyin Guide | Pronunciation, FAQs and more.* Pinyin
Guide. Retrieved December 16, 2020, from
https://www.pinyin-guide.com/

Thought Co. (2019, June 15). *How Did Mandarin Become China's Official
Language?* ThoughtCo.
https://www.thoughtco.com/introduction-to-mandarin-
chinese-
2278430#:~:text=Mandarin%20emerged%20as%20the%20lan
guage

Wei, X. (2020, July 4). *Chinese productions attract global fanbase.* SHINE.
https://www.shine.cn/feature/entertainment/2007041400/

World Data. (n.d.). *Chinese - Worldwide distribution.* Worlddata.Info. Retrieved December 17, 2020, from https://www.worlddata.info/languages/chinese.php

Yi, L. (2013). *Introduction to Chinese Characters | Year of China.* Www.Brown.Edu. https://www.brown.edu/about/administration/international-affairs/year-of-china/language-and-cultural-resources/introduction-chinese-characters/introduction-chinese-characters#:~:text=Oracle%20Bone%20Inscriptions%20refers%20to

All images were created using Krita software.

Made in the USA
Middletown, DE
09 December 2021

54819083R00080